OSPREY COMBAT AIRCRAFT • 60

B-1B LANCER UNITS IN COMBAT

85

SERIES EDITOR: TONY HOLMES

OSPREY COMBAT AIRCRAFT • 60

B-1B LANCER UNITS IN COMBAT

THOMAS WITHINGTON

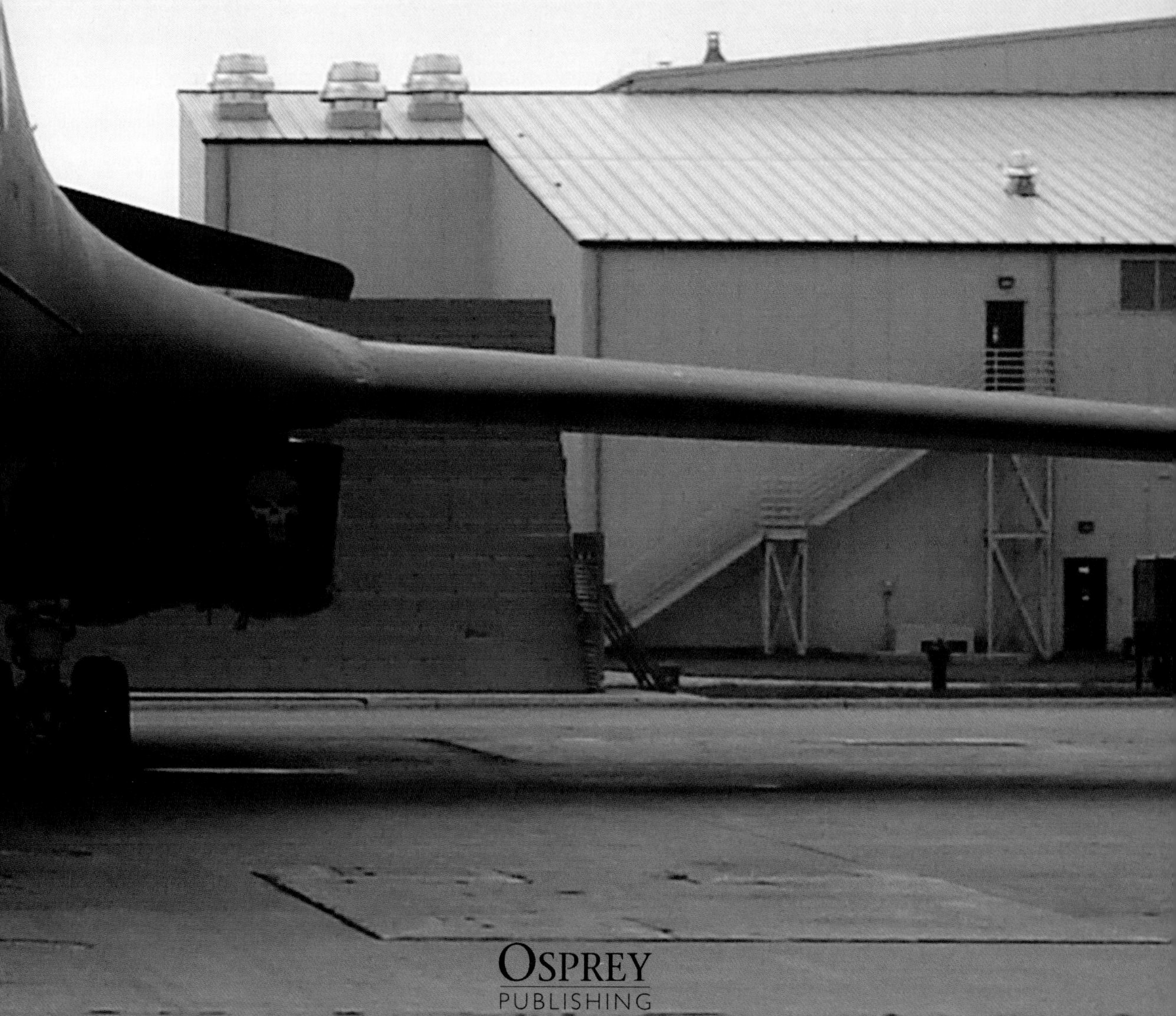

OSPREY
PUBLISHING

Cover caption
During OEF, the B-1B Lancer would not just have to drop weapons to display the aircraft's power – a simple flypast would often suffice. Flying in at low-level and supersonic speeds would often be enough to persuade al-Qaeda or Taleban fighters that a tussle with their Coalition adversaries was simply not worth it. B-1B pilot Capt Richard Morrison of the 37th BS explained that 'the low-altitude pass let the enemy know we were directly overhead, and was usually a morale boost for our troops. We'd come in almost supersonic and it would scare them back into their holes'.

Such flights became more commonplace as the Coalition assisted the Afghan people in their quest to establish a democratic political system throughout the country. 'One story really sticks in my mind from this period', recalled Capt Morrison. He was flying his jet over Afghanistan during a sortie in support of Coalition troops performing anti-Taleban/al-Qaeda operations on the ground in the Spring of 2003.

'We were over Afghanistan and the Combined Air Operations Centre called us up and said "hey, there's this small village, very isolated and the new regional governor is going to arrive" and they asked us for a flyby. So we did a high-speed, low-level pass as the regional governor rode in with a contingent of Afghan National Army soldiers and a squad of US Special Forces guys".'

Capt Morrison explained that such flybys could be challenging for the aircrews, given the country's jagged landscape. 'In certain parts of Afghanistan the terrain is extremely mountainous. There are areas where the aircraft's terrain-following equipment doesn't work so well, and you have to keep that in mind. That was definitely a challenge'. However, the operations in Afghanistan justified Capt Morrison's choice of aircraft. 'I wanted to fly a crew aircraft, but at the same time I wanted to fly something that was tactical and that had a full and meaningful role in combat. That was part of the action, and I always thought the B-1 was so good looking, so fast and so big'
(*Cover artwork by Mark Postlethwaite*)

First published in Great Britain in 2006 by Osprey Publishing
Midland House, West Way, Botley, Oxford, OX2 0PH
443 Park Avenue South, New York, NY 10016, USA

CIP Data for this publication is available from the British Library
ISBN-10 : 1-84176-992-4
ISBN-13 : 978-1-84176-992-9

Edited by Tony Holmes
Page design by Tony Truscott
Cover Artwork by Mark Postlethwaite
Aircraft Profiles by Jim Laurier
Scale Drawings by Mark Styling
Index by Alan Thatcher
Originated by PPS Grasmere, Leeds, UK
Printed and bound in China through Bookbuilders
Typeset in Adobe Garamond, Rockwell and Univers
06 07 08 09 10 11 10 9 8 7 6 5 4 3 2

For a catalogue of all books published by Osprey please contact:
NORTH AMERICA
Osprey Direct, C/o Random House Distribution Center,
400 Hahn Road, Westminster, MD 21157
E-mail:info@ospreydirect.com

ALL OTHER REGIONS
Osprey Direct UK, P.O. Box 140 Wellingborough, Northants, NN8 2FA, UK
E-mail: info@ospreydirect.co.uk
www.ospreypublishing.com

ACKNOWLEDGEMENTS
I am extremely grateful for the generous assistance provided by the following people during the research and writing of this book – Lt Col David 'Gunny' Béen, Commander of the 37th BS; Maj Stephen G Burgh and Capt Josh 'Bert' Nassef of the 7th BW; Capts Kimberley Purdon and Mark Chaisson of the 34th BS; Capts James A 'Famine' Conley, Michael Fessler, Patrick 'Pikey' McMahon, Richard Morrison and Norman Shelton of the 37th BS; Lt Brandon Pollachek, Dyess AFB Public Affairs Office; Lt Elizabeth DeJesus and Senior Airman Jason Piatek at Ellsworth AFB Public Affairs Office; MSgt Dawn L Collazo, Air Combat Command Public Affairs and Media Relations Office; and TSgt Kathleen Cordner, Secretary of the Air Force Office of Public Affairs. Finally, Nathalie Rivére de Carles was both deeply patient and inspirational. Every effort has been made to ensure that this account is as accurate as possible, and responsibility for any errors lies squarely with the author.

CONTENTS

DEVELOPMENT HISTORY

'Good aeroplanes are more important than superiority in numbers' observed Air Vice-Marshal J E 'Johnnie' Johnson, the highest scoring Royal Air Force fighter ace to survive World War 2. His words are more apt today than ever. Despite being deployed in relatively small numbers during Operation *Desert Fox* (ODF) in December 1998, as they would be time and time again in the skies over the Balkans, Afghanistan and Iraq, once again, in 2003, the Boeing/Rockwell International B-1B Lancer has had an incalculable effect on the battlefield, and on the outcome of these conflicts.

The devastating bombardment which the USAF was able to inflict on the likes of the Iraqi regime and its armed forces, Serbian military forces and the rag-tag Taleban militia and its al-Qaeda cohorts was thanks in no small measure to the contribution of the B-1B.

This supersonic, swing-wing bomber conceived in the early 1970s was the result of the 'Advanced Manned Strategic Aircraft' study and was reincarnated in the 1980s to evade enemy radar and to perform nuclear attacks in a superpower confrontation with the Soviet Union and the Warsaw Pact.

Following the collapse of the Berlin Wall in 1989, some pundits had predicted that aircraft such as the B-1B – hugely expensive, technically problematic and designed for a war that, mercifully, never came – would be all but useless for the post-Cold War security environment which would be characterised by 'dirty little wars' in failed or totalitarian states.

A 37th BS B-1B Lancer rolls down the runway at Ellsworth AFB for a training sortie in 2003. The haze aft of the aircraft reveals the power of the F101-GE-102 engines, which are capable of propelling the jet to speeds of Mach 1.25. The Lancer fleet is spread over two bases, with the other facility being at Dyess, in Texas. While the aircraft were deployed with Air National Guard units during the 1990s, they have since been reconsolidated under USAF Air Combat Command (ACC) control. The B-1Bs have also been comprehensively re-roled from nuclear weapons carriers to highly versatile conventional platforms. All of the ACC aircraft underwent the Conventional Munitions Upgrade Program (CMUP) which allowed them to carry weapons such as the GBU-31 JDAM, giving them a potent near precision capability. The ability of the Lancer to deploy JDAM was something which would be increasingly exploited in conflicts in Afghanistan and Iraq (*28th BW*)

The Lancer, thanks in no small part to the dramatic reinvention of the aircraft during the ambitions Conventional Mission Upgrade Program (CMUP), would prove these pundits wrong. Today, the B-1B is an indispensable part of the USAF's heavy bomber fleet, which also includes the B-52H Stratofortress and B-2A Spirit. The Lancer can act as both a strategic heavy bomber as well as a potent Close Air Support (CAS) platform. The aircraft goes from strength-to-strength in every conflict where it participates, becoming more capable and performing more roles as it matures.

B-1Bs 86-0111 and 86-0094 (foreground) from the 37th BS/28th BW at Ellsworth AFB prepare for a training sortie. The B-1B fire training simulator can be seen behind the second aircraft. The DSO/OSO windows, which are situated aft of the cockpit windshield above the wing badge, are also visible (*USAF*)

BIRTH OF THE B-1B

The B-1B Lancer in its present form can trace its routes back to the Rockwell International B-1A bomber developed in the 1970s. This aircraft was later cancelled by President Jimmy Carter in preference to cruise missiles and also, it has since been revealed, for the 'Advanced Technology Bomber' programme which would eventually become the B-2A Spirit stealth bomber. Carter thought that cruise missiles would be much more cost-effective than an expensive manned bomber, and given that the stealth bomber was in development, there seemed to be no sense in having two heavy bomber projects proceeding simultaneously.

The aircraft was resurrected in the early 1980s by President Ronald Reagan, who saw it, among other weapons systems, as a symbolic demonstration to the Soviet Union that his administration was serious about defence and, as history has shown, serious about developing expensive and advanced weaponry. This would force the Soviets to play 'catch up', eventually helping to 'bankrupt' Moscow.

President Carter had cancelled the B-1A on 30 June 1977, but just under five years later, the Reagan administration reactivated the programme. Known initially as the B-1 LRCA (Long Range Combat Aircraft), the bomber would later be officially christened the B-1B Lancer. The aircraft was touted as a cruise missile carrier, although retaining a capability to drop free-fall nuclear weapons. President Reagan made his decision to go ahead with the B-1B in October 1981, with formal contracts for the production of 100 aircraft being signed with Rockwell International on 20 January 1982.

Ready for pushback. A B-1B Lancer of the 37th BS/28th BW is manoeuvred on the ramp at Ellsworth AFB. The outward design of the B-1B differs little from its predecessor, although the cockpit area reveals the main differences between the two aircraft – notably the nose-mounted AN/APQ-164A radar housing, the cockpit windows and the foreplanes (*28th BW*)

Outwardly, both the B-1A prototypes and the B-1B Lancer are very similar in appearance, but that is where the similarity ends. The offensive and defensive avionics (notably the Electronic Counter Measures (ECMs)), radar signature, weapons payload, maximum take-off weight – the B-1A weighs 395,000 lbs (177,750 kg), compared to the B-1B, which weighs 477,000 lb (214,650 kg) – range and speed of the 'Bravo' variant are vastly improved over to the 'Alpha' prototype. These advances in performance took into account technological improvements which had occurred in the intervening years between the development of the two aircraft.

For example, the engine inlets underwent a redesign which eliminated the moveable air ramps used on the 'Alpha's' engine intakes. These were replaced on the 'Bravo' with vanes located within the air intakes, which shielded the engine's fan blades and core from radar signals. Radar Absorbent Materials were also used in the aircraft's construction which led to a reduction in the Radar Cross Section (RCS) for the 'Bravo' by over 85 per cent. Despite being roughly similar in size, it is said that the Lancer has an RCS which is one-fiftieth that of the B-52.

The speeds of the 'Alpha' and the 'Bravo' are also notably different. The B-1A was intended for high-altitude penetration to deliver nuclear weapons, and was therefore designed to fly at Mach 2. The 'Bravo', however, was built for low-altitude missions, and has a maximum speed at low level of around Mach 0.92. The Lancer's maximum speed is thought to be around Mach 1.25.

Outwardly, there are few differences. The B-1B has a small window aft of the cockpit windscreen for the Offensive Systems Operator (OSO) and Defense Systems Operator (DSO). These were installed to make the rear of the crew compartment feel less claustrophobic, although, paradoxically, in flight the blinds that cover the windows are usually left down by the crews so that it is easier for them to see their display screens.

The nose of the aircraft also experienced a slight redesign, which was done to accommodate the AN/APQ-164A multi-mode offensive radar system that was installed for navigation and terrain-following, as well as to get ordnance on target.

One of the most ambitious design features on the 'Alpha' was to have an ejectable crew module in a similar style to that fitted to the F-111, which would jettison the entire crew compartment from the aircraft in the event of an emergency. This was replaced by more conventional ACES II advanced ejection seats, which would be the crew's method of egress. This was done after the crew escape module on a B-1A failed to reposition under its three parachutes following employment in the wake of an in-flight emergency when the jet went out of control. Rockwell International Chief Test Pilot T D Benefield was killed and Maj Richard Reynolds and Capt Otto Waniczek injured when the module made a very heavy landing.

The aft fuselage area behind the Weapons Systems Officers, known as 'Whizzos' from their days in the backseats of F-4 Phantom IIs, was also enlarged to accommodate the increased number of defensive systems which were carried by the 'Bravo'.

The weapons bay in the mid-section of this 28th BW B-1B is occupied by four GBU-31 JDAM. The perforated spoilers which reduce turbulence when the aircraft's ordnance is released can be seen at the front of each weapons bay. The forward weapons bay in this aircraft houses an auxiliary fuel tank to increase the jet's range (*Senior Airman Michael Keller*)

The forward weapons bay of the B-1B has a movable bulkhead to accommodate different sizes of munitions. However, this function has never been used operationally given that the aircraft lost its ability to carry Air-Launched Cruise Missiles (ALCM) as a part of the Strategic Arms Reduction Treaty (START 1) which stipulated that 'a bomber shall not be considered to be a "heavy bomber" if it is not equipped for long-range nuclear ALCMs'. Russian arms inspectors periodically check to ensure that the partition is not moved. A perforated spoiler also folds down from the weapons bay into the aircraft's slipstream during flight to aid the clean release of weapons, and to reduce the turbulence inside the bomb-bay.

The weapons bays can also accommodate auxiliary fuel tanks, and together with the undercarriage housings, they are painted gloss white in order to show up any fluid leakages. Extra fuel tanks can also be installed in the intermediate or aft bays. These tanks carry up to 18,870 lb (8559 kg) of fuel, depending on their design.

LANCER ENTERS SERVICE

The first flight of the B-1B prototype occurred on 23 March 1983. This aircraft, 74-0159, was outfitted with the B-1B avionics systems, but still retained the crew escape module. The first flight of a 'pure' B-1B-configured jet (76-0174) occurred on 30 July 1984. Both of these flights used B-1A airframes fitted out with B-1B offensive and defensive avionics.

Initial service deliveries began less than a year later on 29 June 1985 when aircraft 83-0065 *The Star of ABILENE* was delivered to 96th Bomb Wing (BW) at Dyess Air Force Base (AFB), in Texas, five months ahead of schedule on 4 September 1984. The aircraft performed its maiden flight as part of the wing on 18 October that same year. Meanwhile, the B-1B testing schedule continued, eventually concluding on 31 October 1985.

The B-1B achieved its Initial Operation Capability in July 1986. By 2 May 1988, the last (86-0140) of the 100 Lancers ordered had been delivered. Throughout this production period, B-1Bs were delivered to the USAF ahead of schedule and under budget. Although known

The first B-1B Lancer (83-0065), christened *The Star of ABILENE*, is now an exhibit in the static air park at Dyess AFB. This aircraft was delivered to the USAF on 4 September 1984, and served exclusively with the 9th BS/7th BW until its retirement (*Airman 1st Class Alan Garrison*)

officially as the 'Lancer', the jet is referred to almost exclusively as the 'Bone' (derived from 'B-One') by its crews in the tradition where aircraft are seldom known by their official names in USAF circles.

Despite beating its delivery schedule, the aircraft has been no stranger to controversy, suffering seven losses in 18 years, while problems such as fuel leaks led to the aircraft being grounded on occasions. Particularly temperamental was the jet's AN/ASQ-184 Defensive Avionics System (DAS), which required expensive and regular upgrades. To make matters worse, under-funding of the logistics support for the bomber led to a paucity of spare parts which kept the availability rates of the aircraft low. In 1992-93, for example, just 57 per cent of the fleet was deemed to be mission-capable.

It was also reported that the Lancer 'sat out' the 1991 Gulf War in the Continental United States (CONUS). This was an unfair accusation, for the aircraft was still a nuclear strike platform at the time, and was therefore wedded to the Single Integrated Operational Plan (SIOP) which called for it to provide a nuclear deterrent for the United States, lest the disintegration of the Soviet Union go awry.

Yet the aircraft's relationship with the SIOP was a short one. True, the 'Bone' was more than capable of inflicting an unprecedented amount of nuclear destruction from the air. A nuclear weapons fit could include eight B-61 or B-83 nuclear gravity bombs, or the same number of Lockheed AGM-69B Short-Range Attack Missiles on each Multi-Purpose Rotary Launcher (MPRL). This would have given the aircraft a colossal 28.8 megatons of explosive power if it was fully 'bombed-up' with B-83 weapons – 221 times the destructive power of the 'Little Boy' Hiroshima bomb.

When Operation *Desert Storm* took place the aircraft was yet to undergo the CMUP, and this meant that its conventional capabilities were basic. Meanwhile, its B-52 cousin was more suited to the saturation attacks on Iraqi positions in the Kuwaiti Theatre of Operations and the conventional ALCM strikes that it performed during the conflict (see *Osprey Combat Aircraft 50* for further details).

Nevertheless, availability rates dogged the jet as it failed to reach its 75 per cent mission-capable level until 1994. To cure this deficiency, the USAF decided to conduct an Operational Readiness Assessment (ORA) from 1 June 1994. This would see whether a single B-1B wing could maintain the 75 per cent rate for six months should all of the necessary spare parts, maintenance equipment and personnel be available, and should the logistics system perform properly. By the end of the six-month ORA, the test unit – the 28th BW – achieved an 84.3 per cent mission-capable rate. The 75 per cent figure had been surpassed, but it could not be sustained. The mission-capable

Night maintenance at Ellsworth AFB. The housing for the AN/ALE-50 towed decoy system is located immediately below the tail radome. This defensive system is flanked on either side by the combined AN/ASQ-184 Defensive Countermeasures System, while the AN/ALQ-161A Electronic Countermeasures system is located in the mid-level tail fairing and at the top of the fin (*28th BW*)

One of the four engines fitted to an unidentified Lancer gets a routine maintenance check on the flightline at Ellsworth. The F101-GE-102 engines are notable not just for the awesome power which they generate, but also for their relatively low fuel consumption. The engines are also of a robust, yet compact, design, thus greatly easing maintenance (*28th BW*)

B-1B 85-0085 from the 37th BS/28th BW is towed away from the squadron dispersal area at the end of a training sortie at Ellsworth. The aircraft has all of its weapons bay doors open in preparation for a maintenance inspection. This jet was the 45th B-1B delivered to the USAF. The 28th BW had the distinction of achieving an 83.4 per cent mission capable rate for its aircraft during the B-1B's 1994 Operational Readiness Assessment (*Senior Airman Michael Keller*)

rate for the rest of the 1990s and the beginning of the millennium averaged between 50 and 65 per cent – still well below the 75 per cent goal.

At the same time, the USAF was rethinking the basing of its bombers. B-1B Lancers were deployed with four bomb wings from 1991. The 9th BW was based at Dyess AFB, the 28th BW at Ellsworth AFB, South Dakota, the 384th BW at McConnell AFB, Kansas, and the 319th BW at Grand Forks AFB, North Dakota. In 1994, the USAF moved the 319th BW to McConnell, placing the unit under the jurisdiction of the Air National Guard (ANG). This was the first time that heavy bombers had entered the ANG inventory.

During the Cold War, as ANG personnel could not be continually monitored – a requirement of USAF personnel responsible for nuclear strike missions – they were not permitted to fly heavy bombers. The end of the Cold War and the removal of the aircraft from the SIOP changed this policy. Some 14 Lancers were shared between the 184th BW at McConnell and the 116th BW at Robins AFB, Georgia. All ANG B-1Bs were configured solely for conventional missions. For a time B-1Bs were also assigned to the 366th Air Expeditionary Wing – the USAF's 'pre-packaged' crisis response unit – at Mountain Home AFB, Idaho. The wings at Dyess and Ellsworth had overall responsibility for the Lancer's repair and maintenance.

Today, the B-1B fleet comprises around 60 aircraft, with 30 divided between the 28th BW at Ellsworth, which includes the 77th 'War Eagles' BS, the 34th 'Thunderbirds' BS and the 37th 'Tigers' BS, along with the 7th BW at Dyess, which includes the 9th, 13th and 28th BSs. Also present at this base is the 77th Weapons Detachment,

A 'Bone' from the 37th BS/28th BW thunders aloft from Runway 13/31 at Ellsworth AFB on a cold day in the winter of 2003. This same runway witnessed the crash of 28th BW B-1B 85-0076 on 18 November 1988 when the bomber undershot the runway. All four crew members safely ejected (*28th BW*)

which conducts weapons training and operational evaluation. Some flight continuation training is also performed by the 28th BS.

All B-1B training is completed at the 28th BW's B-1B Flight Training Unit. The latter typically trains ten students each for all four crew positions. The myriad of systems which the 'Whizzos' have to master, along with the highly complex B-1B flight systems which have to be taught to the pilots, results in a demanding course. Training missions are typically six hours in duration, and combine high- and low-altitude bombing runs, tactical formation flying and refuelling.

According to 37th BS pilot Capt Michael Fessler, the course is 'about six months of academic class work mixed in with plenty of flying. Your first month is all academic. You're in the class room almost 12 hours a day. After this, the next five months or so is all flying. You start off with take-offs and landings and basic flying. From there you learn a lot of independent things, like how to refuel with the aircraft, and how to use it as a weapons platform. That's all done at the school house at Dyess AFB. All the very basic stuff is done there. We only learn about specific weapons tactics once we get to our operational squadrons at Ellsworth AFB. They say that at Dyess they teach you how to drive, and once you get to Ellsworth they teach you how to race!'

For fellow 37th BS pilot Capt Richard Morrison, one of the most challenging aspects of flying the aircraft is getting used to the AN/APQ-163 terrain-following radar (TFR);

'Letting the automatic TFR fly the jet is definitely a challenge. You realise that it's a really capable system and it works very well. Traditionally at Dyess they have you go through at least one low-level training flight without night vision goggles, flying with the TFR system, and that's very unnerving. Fortunately, the system works particularly well at night.

'The best thing about this aircraft is that it's very dynamic. It's a very flexible jet, capable of picking up new roles', according to 37th BS instructor 'Whizzo' Capt James 'Famine' Conley. 'However, this dynamism means that there are no set rules which you can follow in terms of working with the aircraft when it comes to teaching new pilots and "Whizzos"'.

By 1992 the B-1B was breaking world records, with two Lancers circumnavigating the globe and performing simulated attacks on bombing ranges in Italy, the Pacific and the CONUS en route. But the fleet would be reorganised once again the next year.

In March 1996 it was announced that the 77th BS would return to Ellsworth. One year later, the 34th BS was transferred to the 366th Wing at Mountain Home AFB. And it was during 1997 that a B-1B from the 7th BW at Dyess flew the very last Lancer SIOP mission. The stage was thus set for the aircraft to become a potent conventional weapons carrier. The USAF went on record at the time stating that the Lancer's strength was its ability to 'penetrate low- to medium-risk threat areas', and that it 'can be easily integrated into composite force packages'.

B-1B 85-0086 *My Mistress* from the 37th BS/28th BW prepares for a night training sortie. During training, student B-1B pilots are expected to perform at least one night sortie without the use of NVGs, instead relying on the aircraft's systems. 85-0086 was retired to AMARC in August 2003 (*Senior Airman Michael Keller*)

As of December 2001, 92 Lancers were in service, although this number has now been reduced to 65 after the USAF took the decision in 2002 to withdraw 32 B-1Bs from frontline use. The balance was distributed between aviation museums and the Aerospace Maintenance and Regeneration Center, more commonly known as the 'Boneyard', at Davis-Monthan AFB, Arizona.

CHARACTERISTICS

The B-1B has a crew of four. The pilot sits in the left-hand seat in the forward crew compartment and the co-pilot sits in the right-hand seat. Behind the pilot is the DSO, while the OSO sits on the right – 'Whizzos' are cross-trained to perform both the DSO and OSO roles. In addition to performing their roles, when flying low-level high-speed missions, the pilot and co-pilot will call out the location of approaching high ground, while the OSO will give its height and the DSO will suggest the best way around it. The cockpit is said to be highly 'user friendly' and noticeably more comfortable than the B-52. Fighter-style 'stick' columns have replaced the yokes which are synonymous with large aircraft. This is highly appropriate given that the handling and performance of the aircraft is closer to that of a fighter than a heavy bomber. One Lancer pilot the author spoke to said that 'sometimes you've got to stop and think how big this aircraft is before you do some things because it handles so well'.

With its wings fully extended, the B-1B has an unmistakeable silhouette that clearly betrays the complexity of the aircraft's surfaces and engine configuration (*28th BW*)

Left
The pilot's station in the B-1B Lancer betrays the 1970s design of the aircraft, and features a stick control column instead of the yoke more usually associated with aircraft of this size (*B-1 Systems Program Office*)

Below
The DSO's station is equipped with several screens detailing the aspect of any threat to the aircraft, along with the appropriate equipment for 'spoofing' the threat (*B-1 Systems Program Office*)

34th BS instructor pilot Capt Mark Chaisson remarked that the aircraft 'handles great, given how heavy and large it is, and going as fast as it does. It's definitely not a lumbering aircraft. When you touch the controls it responds, pretty much giving you the input you asked of it. As far as working with it is concerned, in my opinion it is a dream to fly. It's very smooth, obviously goes very fast and it just doesn't have any issues with acceleration, deceleration, climbing or descending. The variable swept-wings gives us some huge advantages that most aeroplanes lack. In my opinion I think it's just awesome'.

Capt Michael Fessler agreed. 'I've been flying the B-1B since December 2003. It's a blast. It flies a lot like a great big fighter. It's

Left
The OSO's station is equipped with avionics for arming and targeting the Lancer's varied payload. Originally designed for the carriage and delivery of nuclear weapons, these avionics have since been upgraded to work with conventional ordnance (*B-1 Systems Program Office*)

very nimble for a big aeroplane. It's really quick to respond and it's about the fastest thing in the sky for its size'. Capt Richard Morrison commented that 'you don't fly autopilot-coupled approaches in the B-1B – you hand-fly pretty much everything. It's a good combination between high technology and, to some extent, good old "seat-of-the-pants" flying. Most of the money and technology on the airframe has gone into the aft end of the crew compartment, where the "Whizzos" are working'.

The crew workload is greatly assisted by the systems in the aircraft. The cockpit avionics include dual ASN-131 radar altimeters, an inertial navigation system, an APN-218 Doppler radar velocity sensor, an ARN-118 Tactical Air Navigation system and an ARN-108 instrument landing system. The communications suite includes an ASC-19 AFSATCOM (Air Force Satellite Communications System), an ARC-190 High Frequency (HF) radio and KY-58 secure voice line-of-sight encryption device, an APX-101A Identification Friend or Foe system and an ARC-171 Ultra HF line-of-sight radio system.

Most of the aircraft's avionics systems are linked together with quadruple-redundant MIL-STD 1553 data buses, and all of them are hardened to withstand the effects of the Electro Magnetic Pulse which accompanies a nuclear explosion. The aircraft also contains the EMUX or 'Electrical Multiple System'. Dubbed the aircraft's 'spinal column' by Rockwell, the EMUX, which does away with 80 miles of wiring, performs the command and control for many of the aircraft's systems. Such is the complexity of EMUX that it has been christened 'HAL'

A KC-135R from the 319th Air Refueling Wing at Grand Forks AFB, North Dakota, prepares to refuel 77th BS/28th BW B-1B 86-0125 during a sortie over Afghanistan in 2003. Placing the 'Bone's' refuelling receptacle forward of the cockpit windshield gives the pilots a good view of the refuelling procedure, thus increasing the safety margins for both the tanker and the receiver. This is in marked contrast to the B-2A and B-52H, which have their refuelling receptacles which are aft of the cockpit (*Capt Richard Morrison*)

after the conspiratorial computer in Stanley Kubrick's *2001 – A Space Odyssey* film.

The jet's in-flight refuelling socket is positioned in front of the cockpit windscreen to ease the crew's task of lining-up with the tanker during refuelling. The white 'fishbone' pattern atop the nose helps the boom operator 'fly' the tip of the boom into the receptacle during night operations.

The aircraft's distinctive swing-wing arrangement imposes a weight penalty on the Lancer. However, when the wings are extended the jet's range can be appreciably increased and the bomber can operate from much shorter runways. When the wings are swept back, the B-1B is much more stable during high-speed, low-level flight. The minimum sweep angle for the wings is 15 degrees and the maximum 67.5 degrees. The junction between the wing and the fuselage is fitted with an inflatable 'glove' which helps to maintain aerodynamic efficiency, depending on the wing position. Each wing also has seven-segment full-span leading edge slats and six-segment trailing edge flaps which give enhanced lift to shorten take-off runs when the aircraft is fully bombed-up.

The jet's Fuel and Center of Gravity Management Subsystem (FCGMS) enables it to stay aerodynamically efficient by shifting fuel from one tank to another when the aircraft changes wing position. This has the effect of minimising the increased drag which is experienced at transonic speeds of between Mach 0.85 and Mach 0.9.

Fuel management is one of the most critical aspects to the bomber, with the 'Bone's' fuel load being distributed across eight tanks. Each wing houses a single fuel tank, while the fuselage has six fuel storage areas. However, as the Lancer is a variable-geometry aircraft, the airframe's Centre of Gravity (CG) can be radically altered as the wings change position. This can in turn change the aircraft's attitude, with potentially disastrous results.

During in-flight refuelling, fuel is distributed to all eight tanks, but when the forward fuselage tank is full, this can affect the aircraft's CG. Therefore, the FCGMS opens and closes the valves of the forward tank to ensure the aircraft's stability as it refuels. Interestingly, the clean, flat underside of the bomber gives the aircraft 'lifting body' characteristics, improving its fuel burn performance. Fuel is also used as a cooling source for the significant heat which is generated by the jet's avionics.

Although the B-1B is powered by four General Electric F101-GE-102 engines, which can each produce up to 30,780 lbs of afterburning thrust, the aircraft can fly on two engines or even a single powerplant, providing that the crew dump fuel from the bomber. The jet is also fitted with an Auxiliary Power Unit (APU) which can be used to start the engines should a rapid egress be necessary. A single APU can start all four of the bomber's engines, and a switch to activate the APU is positioned on the front nose-wheel to allow this to be done if the aircrew are not yet in the cockpit.

In terms of the offensive and defensive avionics, the AN/APQ-164A multimode radar is the primary offensive avionics instrument, and it is operated by the OSO. The system has a low-observable phased-array antenna for low-altitude terrain following, and also provides accurate

A Bone from the 37th BS/28th BW shows off the dramatic forward sweep of the Lancer's wings, which give the aircraft a reduced take-off run and greater range. The leading-edge slats on the wings are clearly visible, along with sleek shape of the 'Bone', which goes a long way to decreasing the aircraft's radar signature (*28th BW*)

navigational data for the aircraft. The AN/APQ-164A was developed from the AN/APG-66 system which was fitted in the F-16 Fighting Falcon.

The radar is designed to provide single 'snapshots' of targets or, alternatively, to perform partial radar sweeps. The radar has 11 operating modes to allow for terrain-following flight. This enables the aircraft to fly two distinct low-altitude profiles. The Terrain Following (TER FLW) function gives pilot inputs for pitch steering control during low level flight. The Terrain Avoidance (TER AVD) mode provides the crew with information on obstacles which they may encounter protruding above the aircraft's altitude during low-level flights. The TER AVD function also shows the crew areas of intense electronic countermeasure activity, along with precipitation and the horizontal profile of the terrain at any given point on the horizon.

In addition, the radar also provides information for tanker rendezvous, and is fitted with a Synthetic Aperture Radar (SAR) imaging function which allows the OSO to detect the bomber's targets through heavy cloud and precipitation.

The DSO, meanwhile, uses the AN/ASQ-184 DCS which comprises the Eaton AN/ALQ-161A Electronic Countermeasures System (ECMS) receiver/jammer unit – this can be seen in its housing atop the aircraft's tail fin. This automatically controls jamming functions such as the dispersal of chaff and flares from the accompanying Expendable Countermeasures system. The latter includes eight chaff and flare dispensers which can hold either 12 flares or 120 chaff cartridges. The DCS has a reprogrammable design to allow it to accommodate changing or new threats. All of this provides the aircraft with 360-degree threat coverage.

The DCS will only react when it needs to, thus not giving away the bomber's position by emitting electronic signals. Moreover, the system sorts the threats into highest-priority order, and jamming signals are only emitted in a certain direction, and for only a short time, again so as not to betray the Lancer's position.

In terms of offensive systems, a total of 75,000 lbs (34,020 kgs) of weapons can be carried in the aircraft's three weapons bays – two aft of the cockpit and one aft of the wing box. The first conventional weapon which the B-1B received clearance to carry was the Mk 82 500-lb unguided gravity bomb. This weapon was subsequently used to great effect during Operation *Noble Anvil* (ONA) – the US contribution to NATO's Operation *Allied Force* against Serbia in 1999.

The Mk 82 comes in three different guises according to the fin sets which are installed on the weapon. 'Slick' conical fins can be fitted to give the bomb a low-drag profile, while 'Snakeye' retarded fins slow the bomb down. Finally, the BSU-49 'Air-Inflatable Retard' (AIR) tail

Maintenance personnel from the 28th BW perform checks on the defensive systems of Lancer 85-0085. The countermeasures installed on the aircraft are highly complex, and they initially caused some major headaches for maintainers (*Senior Airman Michael Keller*)

gives the weapon a variable high- or low-drag mode. The BSU-49's configuration can be selected in flight by the OSO.

One of the Mk 82 derivatives was the Mk 62 'Quick Strike' sea mine. Although the sea mine capability has never been used by the Lancer in combat, the 'Bone' can carry 84 of these weapons, which have a drag parachute to slow the weapon down as it is released from the aircraft towards the water. The sea mines can be used in waters up to 300-ft deep.

Until 1995, the Mk 82 was the only conventional bomb which was certified for use by the 'Bone'. However, that year saw the 28th BW commence trials of the Lancer/Mk 84 2000-lb bomb combination, and the jet was duly cleared to carry the ordnance.

These weapons are carried on a rotating 'clip' known as the Conventional Rotary Launcher (CRL). Each CRL can carry up to 28 munitions depending on their size, giving the bomber a total load of 84 weapons. The bomber is also equipped with eight under-fuselage hardpoints which could carry an additional 59,000 lbs (26,750 kg) of weapons, although arms control treaties ensure that munitions are not affixed to these hardpoints.

These external stations were originally installed to allow the jet to carry Boeing AGM-86B nuclear ALCMs. However, due to geopolitical events, and accompanying arms control measures, the missiles were never carried on the aircraft. The ALCMs had the added effect of greatly enlarging the Lancer's RCS, which would have degraded one of the aircraft's greatest attributes – its low observability.

The CMUP enabled the B-1B Lancer to carry several new weapons systems, including the GBU-31 JDAM, two of which are loaded on this Conventional Rotary Launcher ready to be installed in the weapons bay of a 28th BW B-1B (*28th BW*)

CMUP

The B-1B's impressive payload made it particularly attractive as a conventional bomber once the Cold War concluded. This caused the USAF to consider improving the aircraft's conventional capabilities through the CMUP, which was initiated in 1993. This $2.7-billion project manifested itself as a series of Block upgrades to the aircraft. All pre-CMUP jets were designated B-1B Block As, their designations changing as their capabilities were improved. The CMUP was also made possible by arms control agreements between Russia and the

United States, which stipulated that each party to the START II treaty could re-orientate 100 heavy bombers from nuclear to conventional missions, although such aircraft were required to be at segregated facilities away from nuclear air bases. Moreover, such aircraft, and their crews, were barred from participating in nuclear missions or nuclear exercises. Finally the aircraft had to be visibly different to the heavy bombers still designated for nuclear missions, hence the weapons bay partition.

The first stage of the CMUP was the Block B upgrade. This improved the aircraft's existing offensive system, notably the SAR abilities of the AN/APQ-164A and the DCS, to reduce the number of 'false alarms' that the system would generate. Block B modifications were completed across the fleet in 1995.

Predictably, Block B was then followed by Block C. The latter allowed the jet to carry a range of cluster munitions after their CRLs were modified and the aircraft's offensive systems were furnished with the necessary software to deliver CBU-87, -88 and -97 cluster weapons. This upgrade was initiated in 1995 and completed in September 1997.

The CBU-87 Combined Effects Munition comprises 202 bomblets housed inside the weapon's casing. A tail-mounted 'Ballute' inflatable parachute is fitted, along with an anti-materiel shaped charge in the nose of the bomblet. Once the weapon (*text continues on page 33*)

419th Flight Test Squadron B-1B 85-0068 unleashes its load of cluster munitions over the Edwards AFB Precision Impact Range Area in the mid 1990s during early testing of the CBU-87. A T-38A from the 412th Test Wing acts as a chase aeroplane behind the bomber. 85-0068 has served with the test squadron at Edwards since its delivery to the USAF in the late 1980s. The Lancer is equipped with radar and inertial navigation equipment which enables its crew to globally navigate and update mission profiles and target coordinates in-flight, as well as precision bomb, without the need for ground-based navigation aids (*USAF*)

COLOUR PLATES

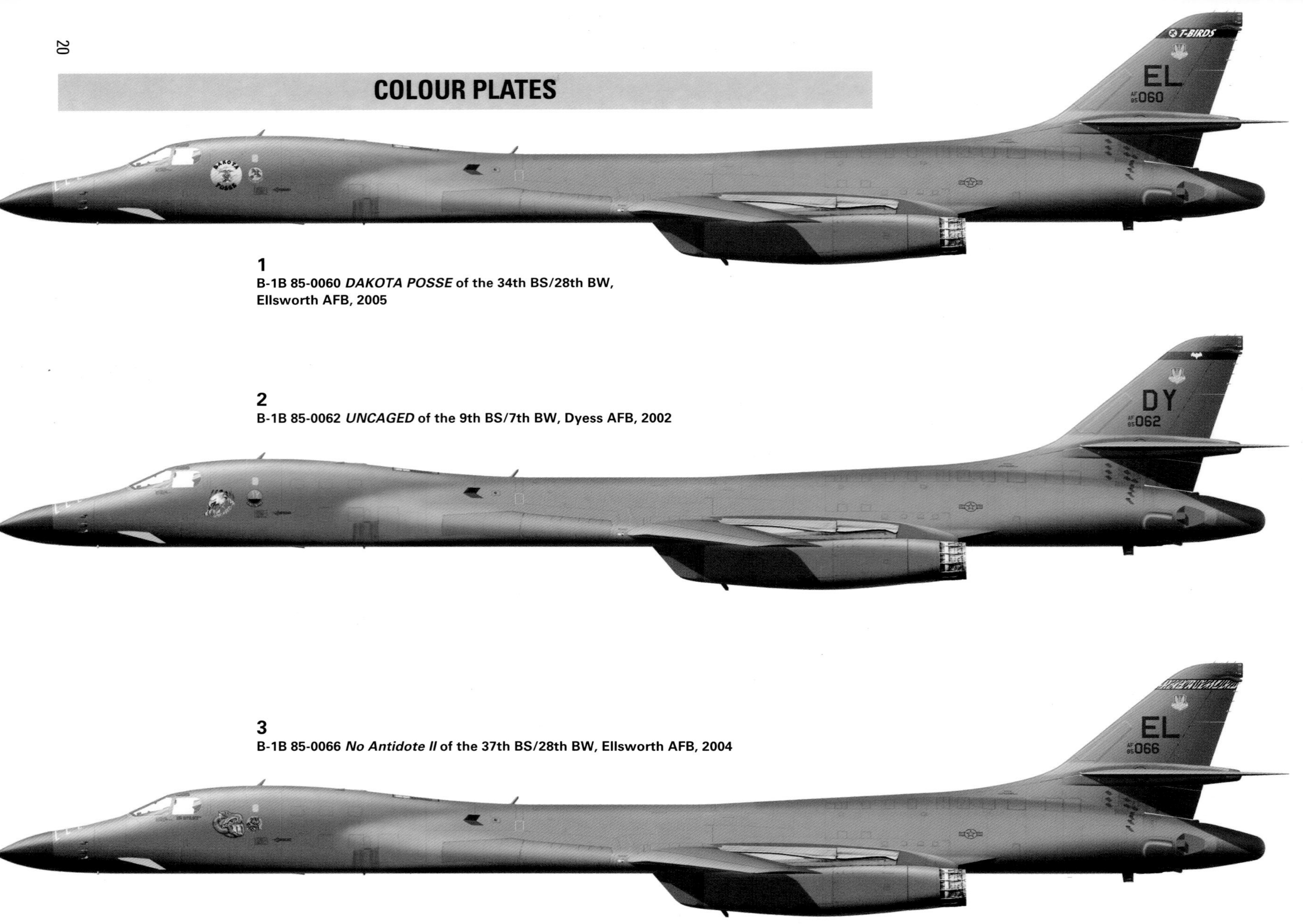

1
B-1B 85-0060 *DAKOTA POSSE* of the 34th BS/28th BW, Ellsworth AFB, 2005

2
B-1B 85-0062 *UNCAGED* of the 9th BS/7th BW, Dyess AFB, 2002

3
B-1B 85-0066 *No Antidote II* of the 37th BS/28th BW, Ellsworth AFB, 2004

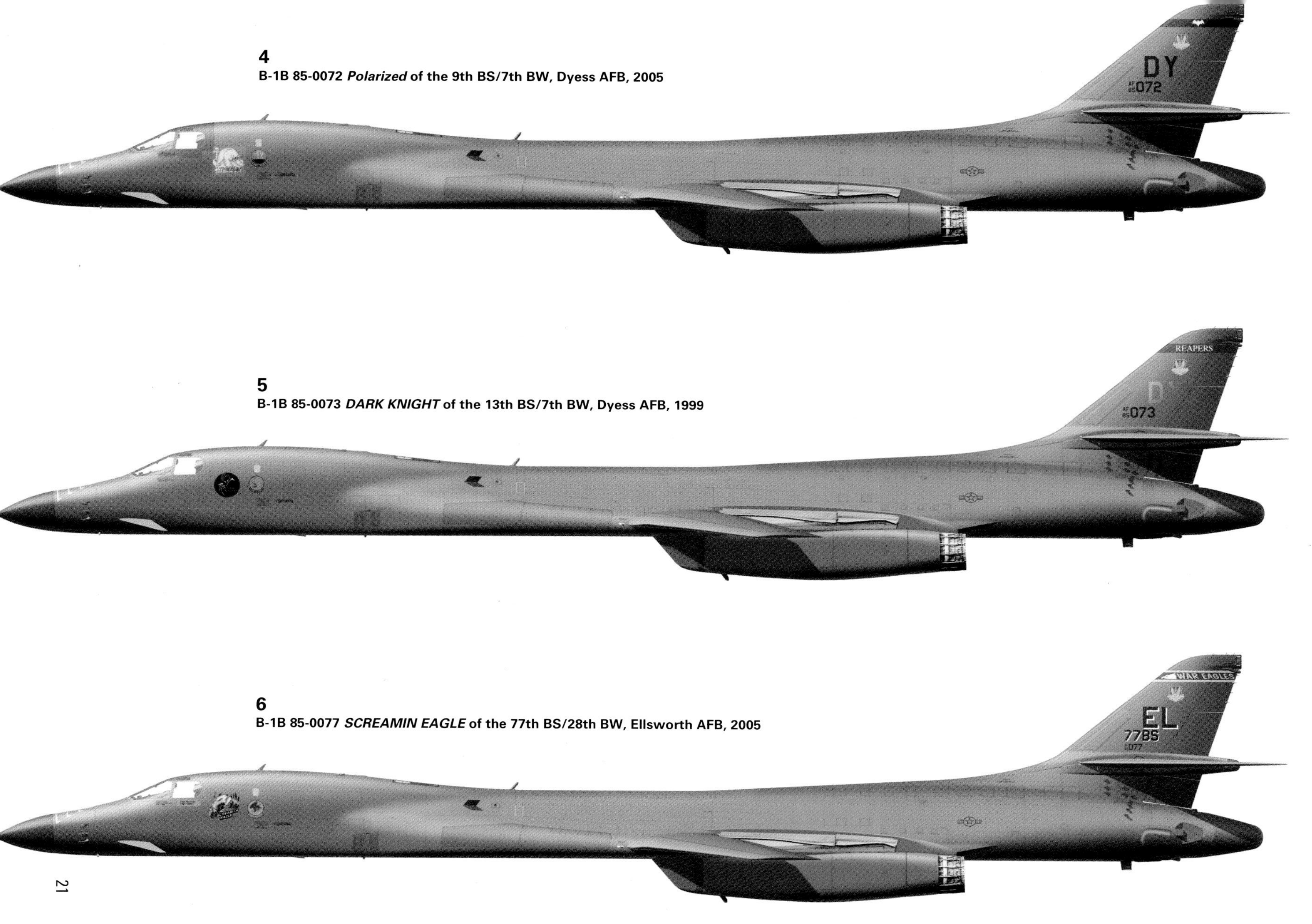

4

B-1B 85-0072 *Polarized* of the 9th BS/7th BW, Dyess AFB, 2005

5

B-1B 85-0073 *DARK KNIGHT* of the 13th BS/7th BW, Dyess AFB, 1999

6

B-1B 85-0077 *SCREAMIN EAGLE* of the 77th BS/28th BW, Ellsworth AFB, 2005

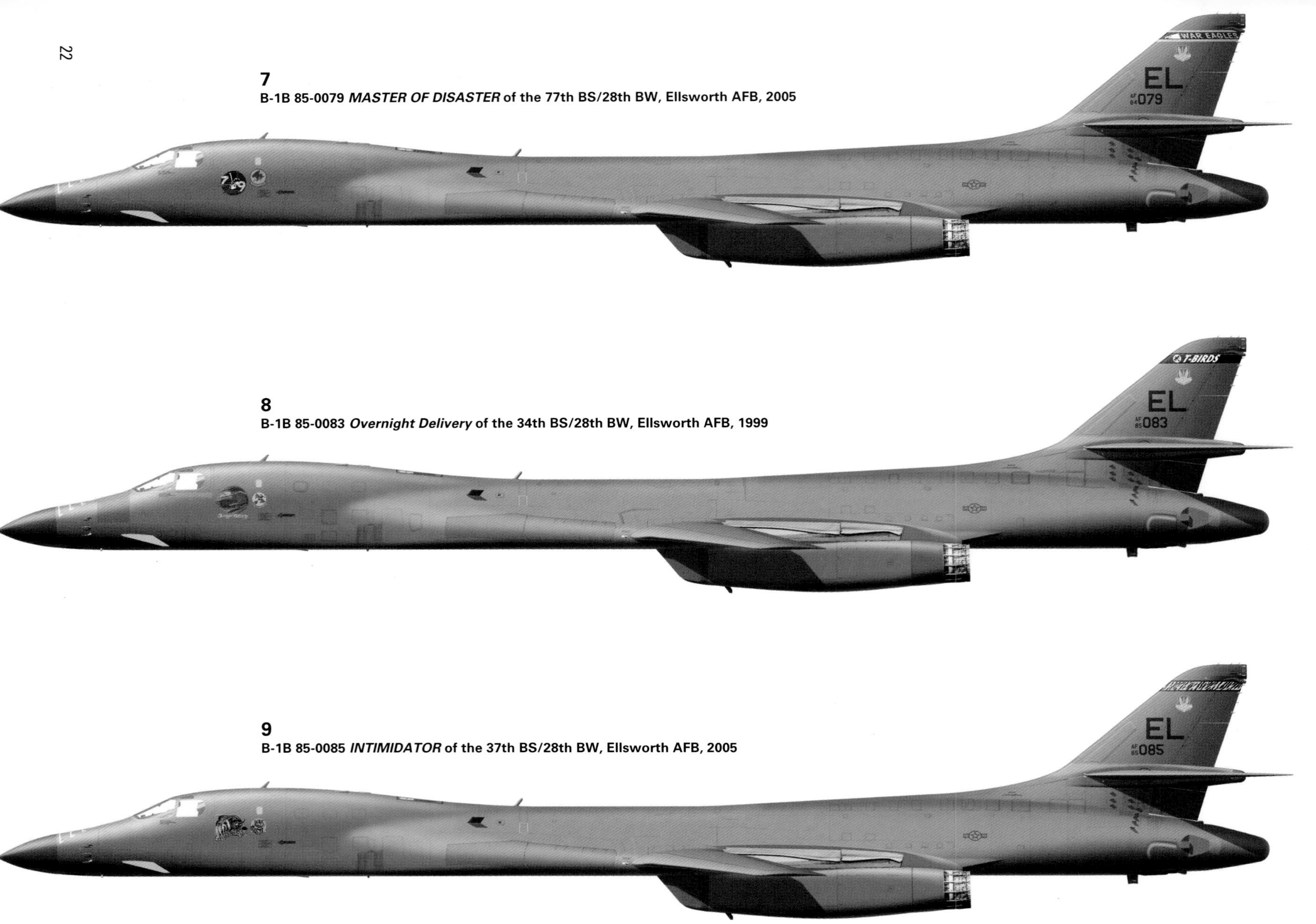

7
B-1B 85-0079 *MASTER OF DISASTER* of the 77th BS/28th BW, Ellsworth AFB, 2005

8
B-1B 85-0083 *Overnight Delivery* of the 34th BS/28th BW, Ellsworth AFB, 1999

9
B-1B 85-0085 *INTIMIDATOR* of the 37th BS/28th BW, Ellsworth AFB, 2005

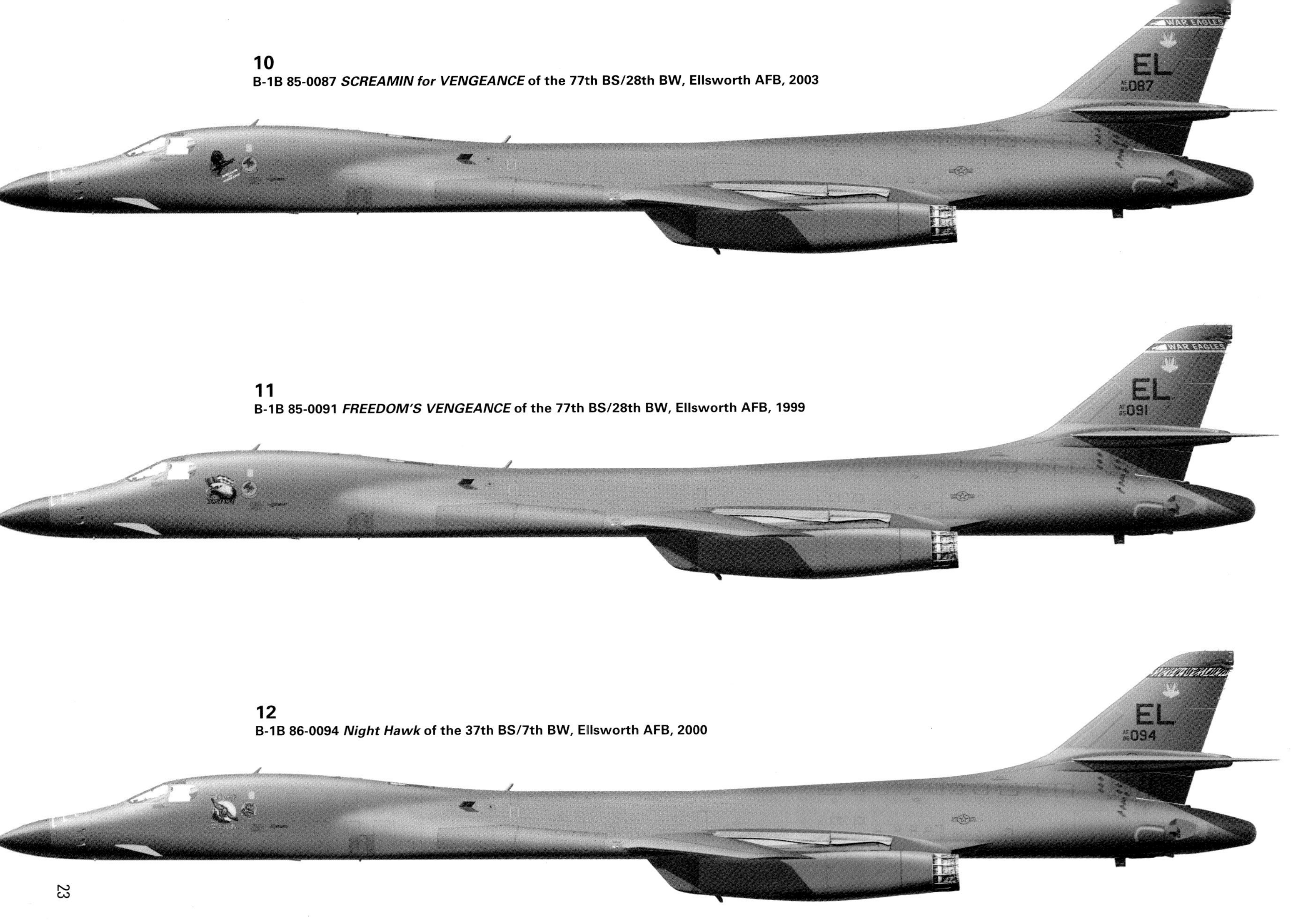

10
B-1B 85-0087 ***SCREAMIN for VENGEANCE*** of the 77th BS/28th BW, Ellsworth AFB, 2003

11
B-1B 85-0091 ***FREEDOM'S VENGEANCE*** of the 77th BS/28th BW, Ellsworth AFB, 1999

12
B-1B 86-0094 ***Night Hawk*** of the 37th BS/7th BW, Ellsworth AFB, 2000

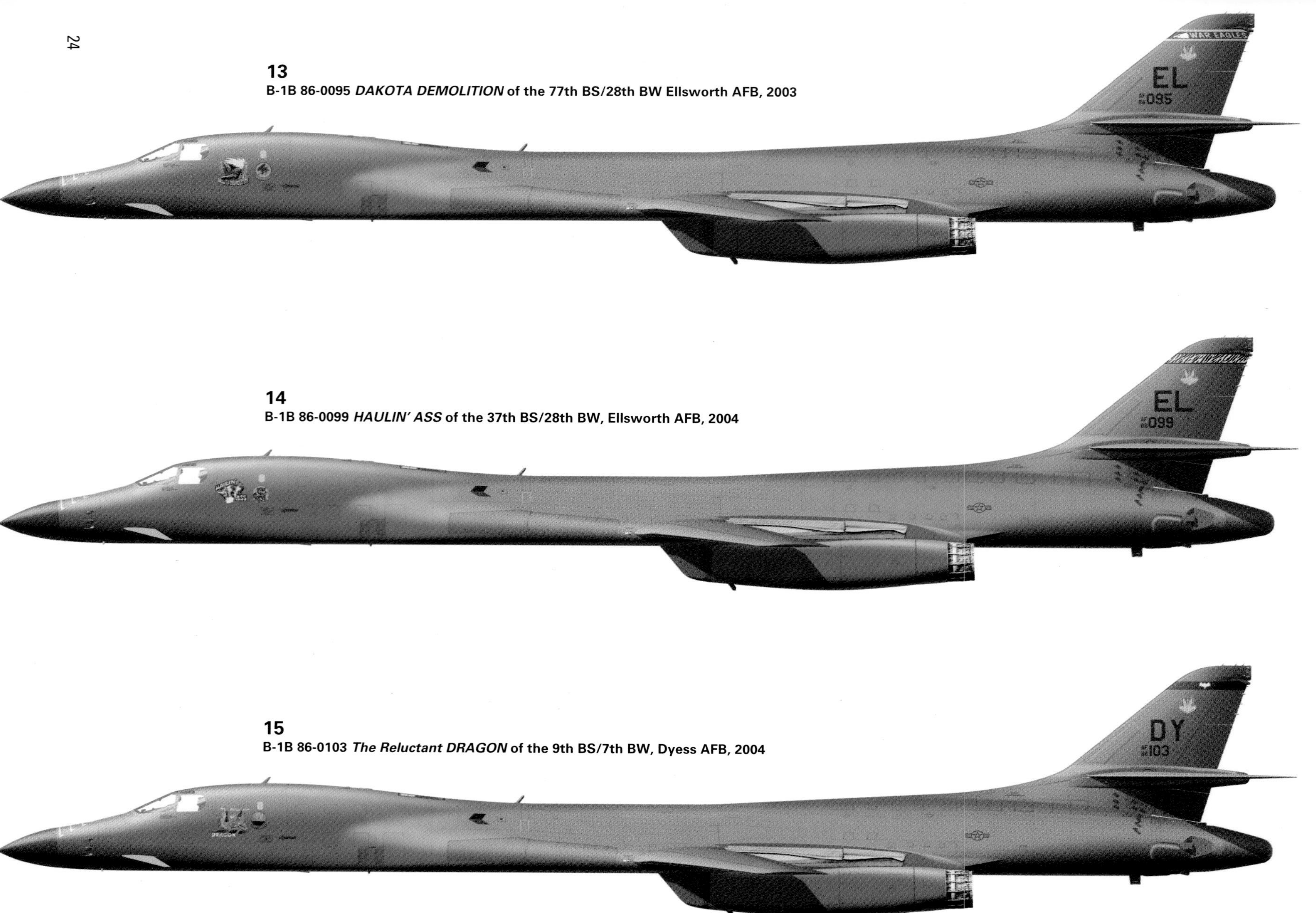

13
B-1B 86-0095 *DAKOTA DEMOLITION* of the 77th BS/28th BW Ellsworth AFB, 2003

14
B-1B 86-0099 *HAULIN' ASS* of the 37th BS/28th BW, Ellsworth AFB, 2004

15
B-1B 86-0103 *The Reluctant DRAGON* of the 9th BS/7th BW, Dyess AFB, 2004

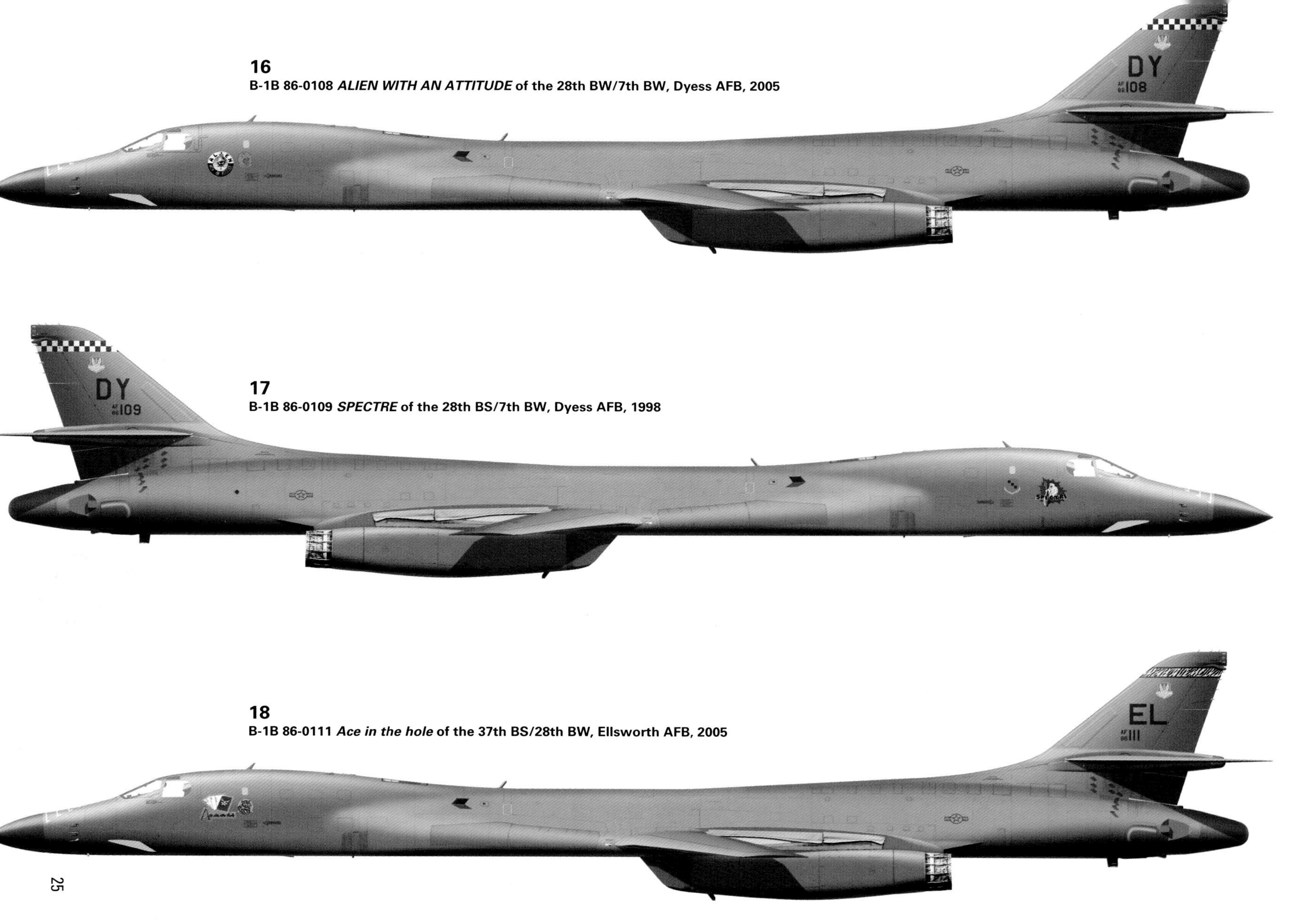

16
B-1B 86-0108 *ALIEN WITH AN ATTITUDE* of the 28th BW/7th BW, Dyess AFB, 2005

17
B-1B 86-0109 *SPECTRE* of the 28th BS/7th BW, Dyess AFB, 1998

18
B-1B 86-0111 *Ace in the hole* of the 37th BS/28th BW, Ellsworth AFB, 2005

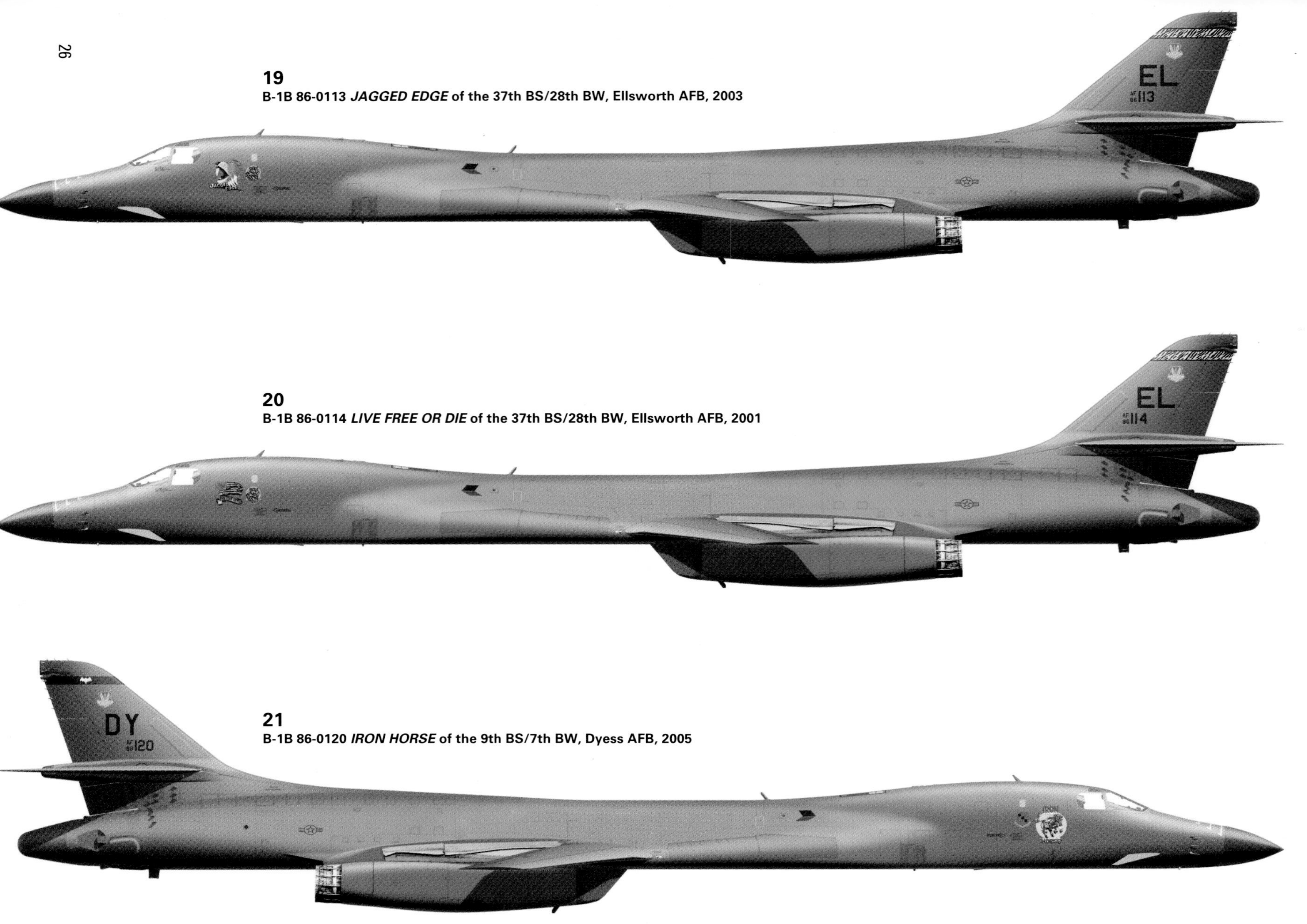

19
B-1B 86-0113 *JAGGED EDGE* of the 37th BS/28th BW, Ellsworth AFB, 2003

20
B-1B 86-0114 *LIVE FREE OR DIE* of the 37th BS/28th BW, Ellsworth AFB, 2001

21
B-1B 86-0120 *IRON HORSE* of the 9th BS/7th BW, Dyess AFB, 2005

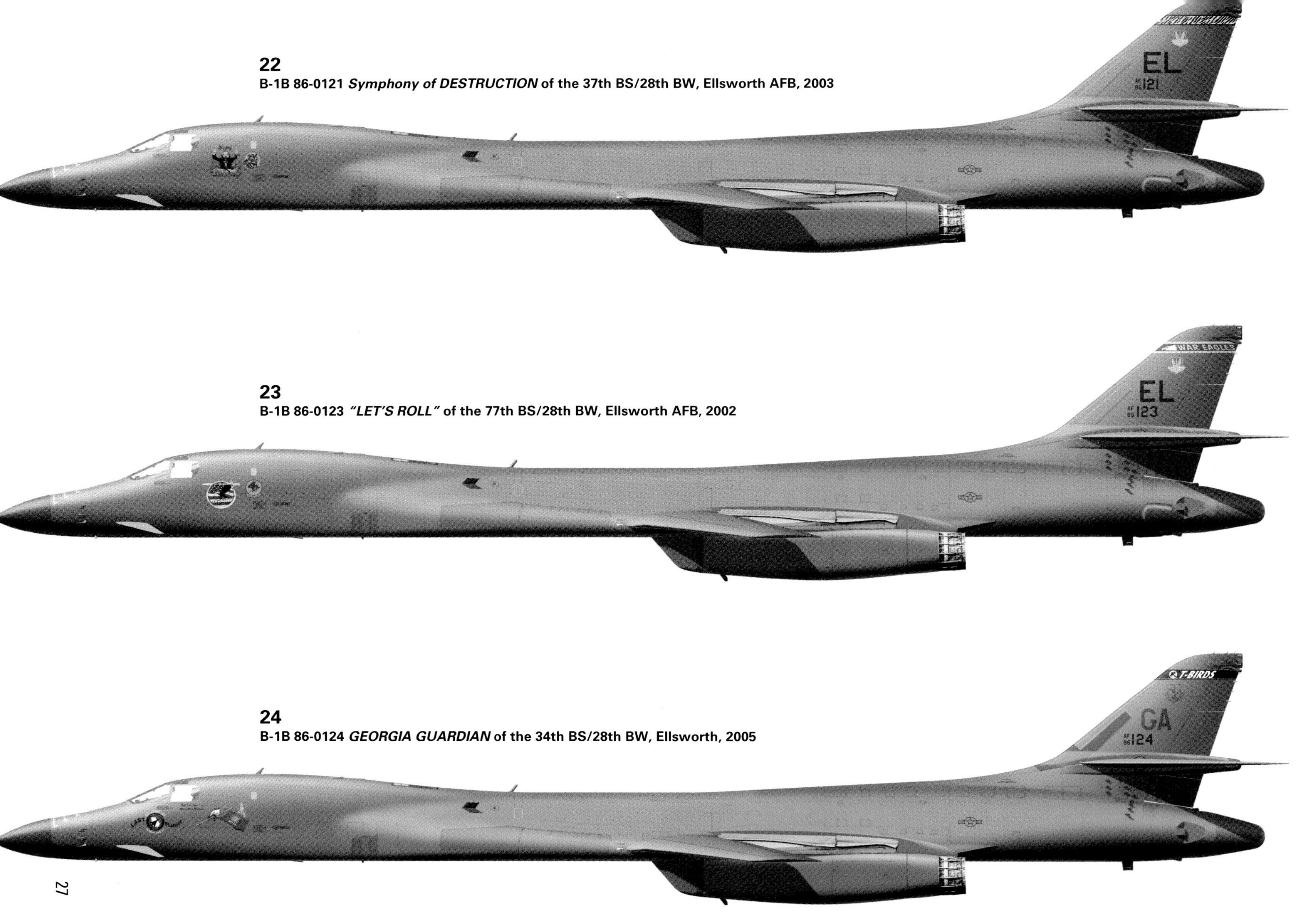

22
B-1B 86-0121 *Symphony of DESTRUCTION* of the 37th BS/28th BW, Ellsworth AFB, 2003

23
B-1B 86-0123 *"LET'S ROLL"* of the 77th BS/28th BW, Ellsworth AFB, 2002

24
B-1B 86-0124 *GEORGIA GUARDIAN* of the 34th BS/28th BW, Ellsworth, 2005

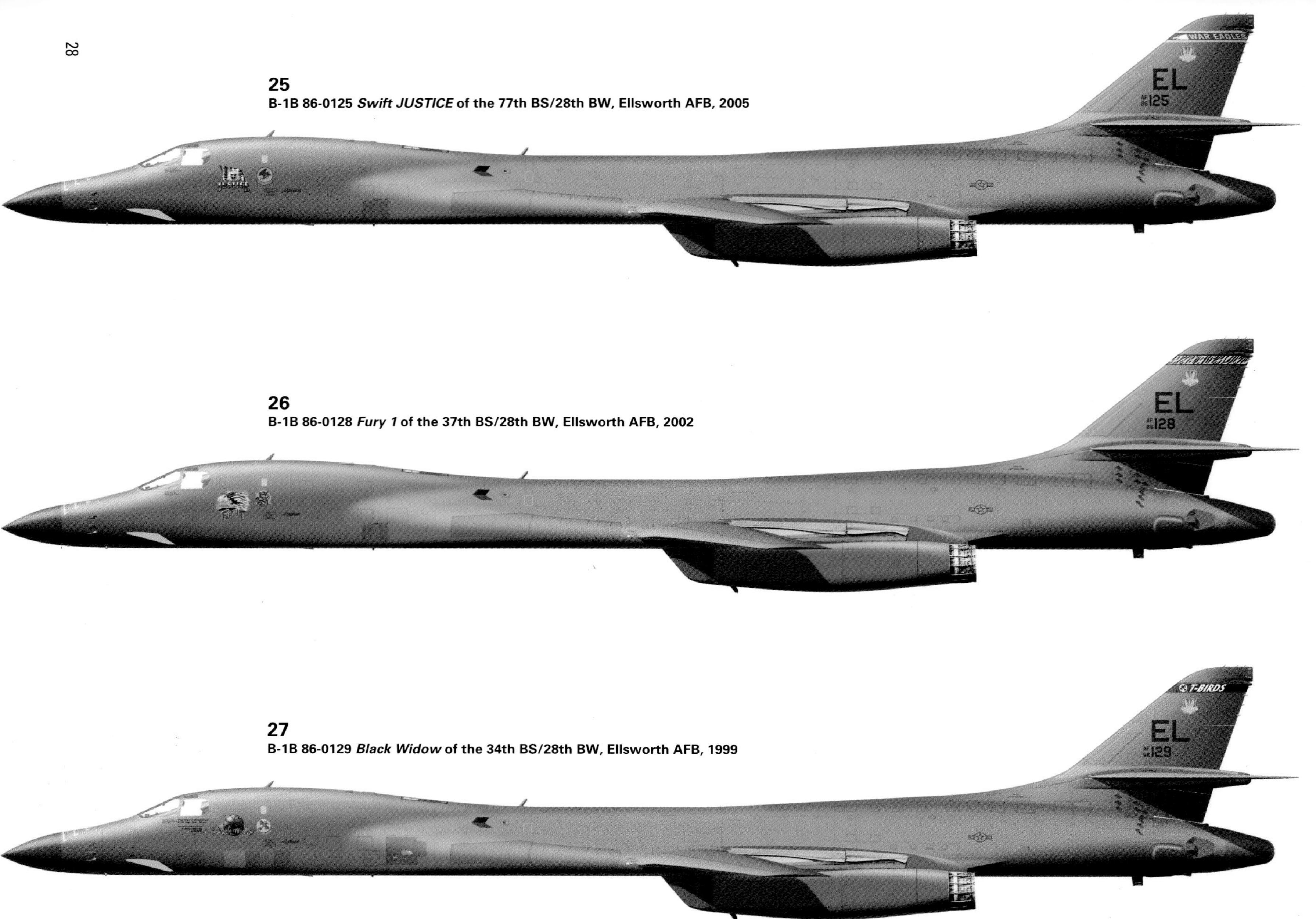

25
B-1B 86-0125 *Swift JUSTICE* of the 77th BS/28th BW, Ellsworth AFB, 2005

26
B-1B 86-0128 *Fury 1* of the 37th BS/28th BW, Ellsworth AFB, 2002

27
B-1B 86-0129 *Black Widow* of the 34th BS/28th BW, Ellsworth AFB, 1999

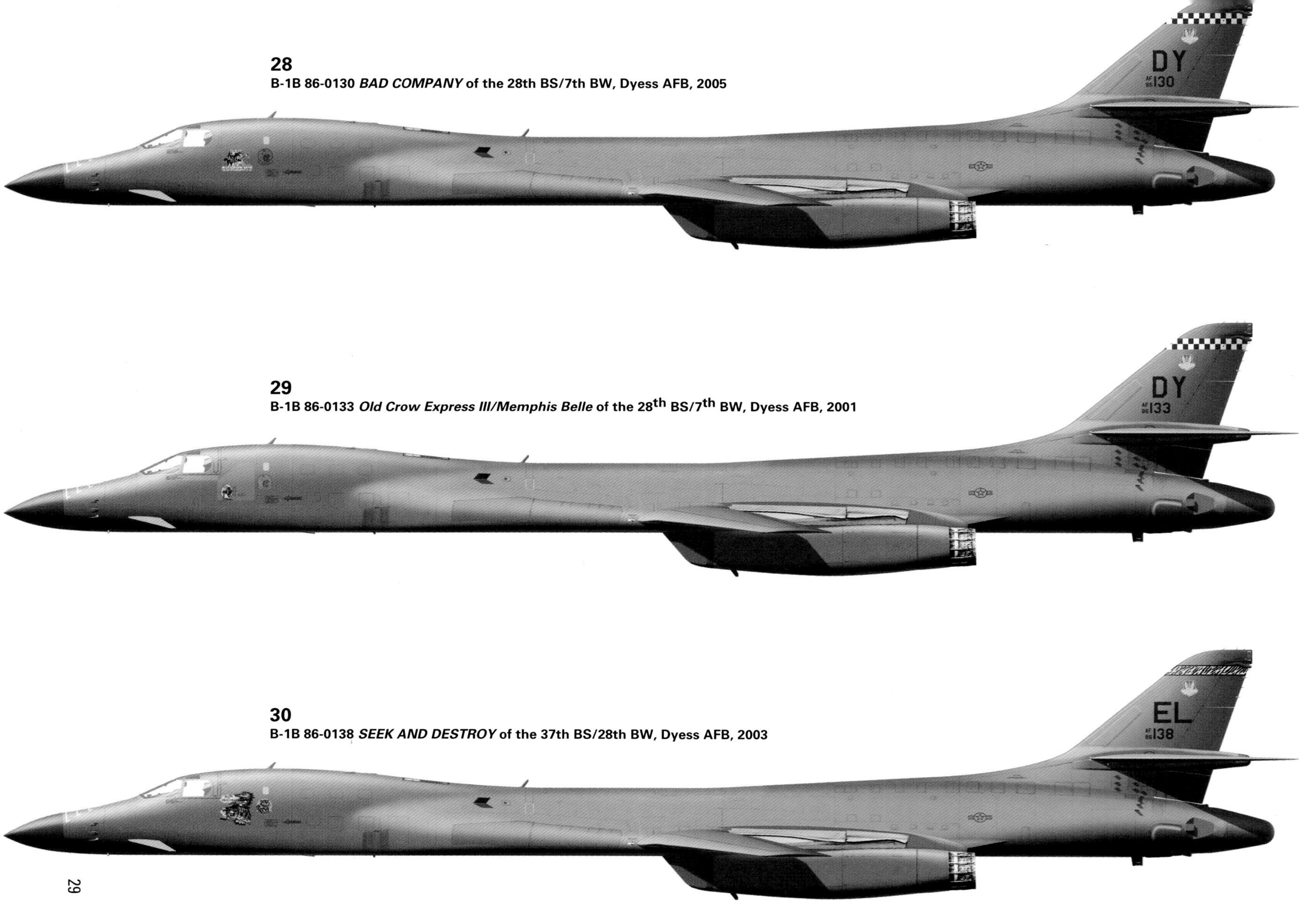

28
B-1B 86-0130 *BAD COMPANY* of the 28th BS/7th BW, Dyess AFB, 2005

29
B-1B 86-0133 *Old Crow Express III/Memphis Belle* of the 28th BS/7th BW, Dyess AFB, 2001

30
B-1B 86-0138 *SEEK AND DESTROY* of the 37th BS/28th BW, Dyess AFB, 2003

Colour Nose/Tail Art Gallery

FREEDOMS VENGEANCE
77th BOMB SQUADRON
Night Hawk
37th BOMB SQUADRON
DAKOTA DEMOLITION
77th BOMB SQUADRON
HAULIN' ASS
37th BOMB SQUADRON
The Reluctant DRAGON
9th BOMB SQDN
ALIEN WITH AN ATTITUDE
Ace in the hole
37th BOMB SQUADRON
JAGGED EDGE
37th BOMB SQUADRON
LIVE FREE OR DIE
37th BOMB SQUADRON
1. PUSH BUTTON TO OPEN DOOR 2. PRESS RELEASE BAR 3. PULL HANDLE OUT TO JETTISON UPPER HATCH 4. DO NOT FACE HATCH
SPECTRE
AIR COMBAT COMMAND

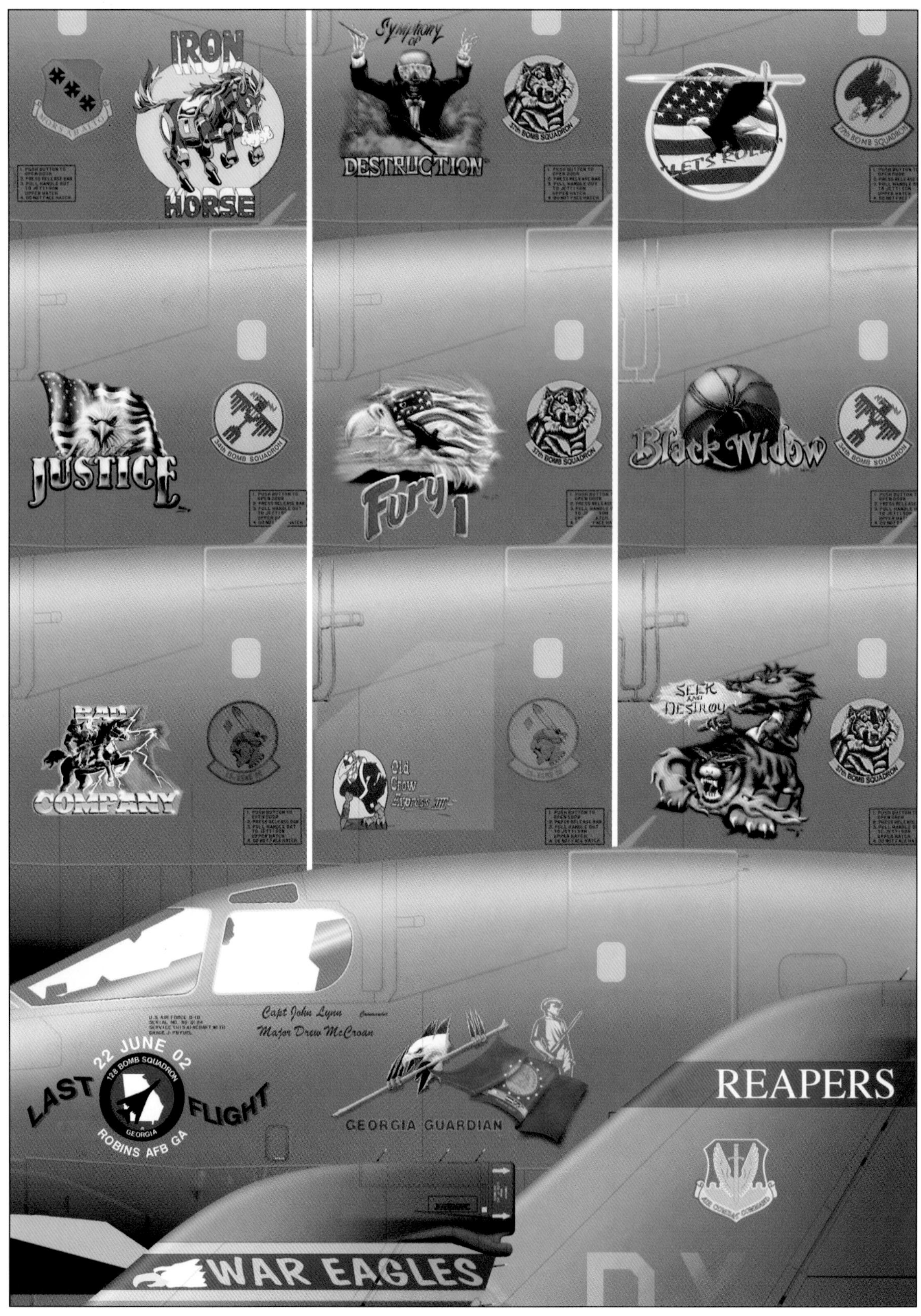
IRON HORSE
Symphony of DESTRUCTION
37th BOMB SQUADRON
LET'S ROLL
77th BOMB SQUADRON
JUSTICE
34th BOMB SQUADRON
Fury 1
37th BOMB SQUADRON
Black Widow
34th BOMB SQUADRON
BAD COMPANY
Old Crow Express III
SEEK AND DESTROY
37th BOMB SQUADRON
Capt John Lynn
Major Drew McCroan
22 JUNE 02
128 BOMB SQUADRON
GEORGIA
ROBINS AFB GA
LAST FLIGHT
GEORGIA GUARDIAN
REAPERS
WAR EAGLES

explodes, the casing disintegrates, dispersing anti-personnel fragments. Each B-1B can carry 30 CBU-87s, with ten in each weapons bay.

The CBU-89 'Gator' is a more robust version of the CBU-87. This weapon has 22 BLU-91/B anti-tank mines, along with 22 BLU-92/B anti-personnel mines, within each canister. Once the weapon has been dropped and the mines have been dispersed on the ground, the latters' FZU-39/B proximity sensor will detect armour and detonate at the best range. The anti-personnel mines lie in wait for any sappers who arrive to try and clear a path through the BLU-91/Bs.

However, far and away the most sophisticated, and expensive, CBU cleared for use by the Lancer is the CBU-97 Sensor Fused Weapon (SFW). At $300,000 per unit, the SFW is not cheap, and a combined load of 30 could cost upwards of $10 million.

Designed with the B-1B's battlefield interdiction role in mind, and intended to devastate a column of armoured vehicles, each CBU-97 consists of a SUU-66/B Tactical Munitions Dispenser which is fitted with a radar altimeter that triggers the release of ten parachute-stabilised BLU-108/B sub-munitions at a specific altitude. Each of the latter contains five Skeet armour-penetrating projectiles, which are outfitted with an infrared (IR) seeker to detect a vehicle by its heat source – principally the engine. It then fires a shaped charge penetrator at the top of the vehicle. Should that vehicle be a tank, then the soft armour on the roof of the turret is targeted by the Skeet.

The Block D upgrade, which was initiated in 1995 and was completed in 2003, saw the B-1B adapted to carry the GBU-31 Joint Direct Attack Munition (JDAM) weapons system – 24 per aircraft in total – in addition to adding new countermeasures such as the AN/ALE-50 Towed Decoy System. The latter produces a bigger, and therefore more tempting, radar signature behind the bomber to 'seduce' anti-aircraft missiles away from the jet. Improvements to the communications system were also installed, making them more resistant to jamming. According to the USAF, the modification gave the aircraft a 'near-precision' attack capability, which would make the B-1B highly suited to operations in the Balkans, Afghanistan and Iraq.

The Lancer-JDAM mix has proven to be the seminal weapons combination for the B-1B in combat. The JDAM was not technically a weapon in its own right. Instead, it was an adapter tail and body strake system which could be fitted onto the Mk 82/83/84 unguided bombs. The JDAM tail kit contains a Global Positioning System (GPS) and Inertial Navigation Systems (INS) which can be programmed with coordinates from the Lancer's GPS receiver.

Other improvements to the aircraft to allow it to be JDAM-compatible included the addition of a MIL-STD 1760 'smart weapons' interface which allowed these coordinates to be downloaded from the aircraft's offensive systems to the JDAM. A Lancer can carry 24 JDAM, each of which can land within 45 ft (13.7-m) of its target when guided by GPS. Even being used in the INS mode, the accuracy of the weapon is within around 100-ft (30.4-m) of the target.

The bombs are deployed from the MPRL, which was previously used to carry nuclear weapons. Both the MPRL and the CRL are 'slotted' into the aircraft's weapons bays on the ground, pre-fitted with

the munitions which will be used in the mission.

US Congress fortuitously provided extra funding during the Block D programme to allow seven aircraft to complete the upgrade 18 months ahead of schedule. By December 1998 three jets had been completed, with the last four upgraded aircraft being delivered back to the 28th BW at Ellsworth AFB in February 1999 – just in time to participate in ONA. By January 2000, seven Block D aircraft had been delivered to the 7th BW at Dyess.

Three GBU-31 JDAM are loaded onto the CRL in the mid-section weapons bay of this Lancer while a member of the flightcrew and one of the aircraft's maintainers perform an inspection of the aircraft at Ellsworth AFB. The Mk 82 section of the weapon can be seen with its green and tarnished bomb case. The grey fairings which have been added to the bombs are the Global Positioning System guidance unit, which is located in the tail, and the strakes, which improve the weapon's aerodynamics (*Senior Airman Michael Keller*)

Further enhancements were made to the aircraft's conventional abilities via the Block E upgrade, which was scheduled for completion in 2005. These changes allowed the Lancer to deploy a larger range of conventional munitions, including the Wind-Corrected Munitions Dispenser (WCMD), the AGM-154A Joint Stand-Off Weapon (JSOW) and AGM-158 Joint Air-to-Surface Stand-Off Munition (JASSM).

JSOW can be launched 17 miles from the bomber's target when flying at low altitude, or at 46 miles on a high altitude attack. Like JDAM, JSOW uses either a GPS or INS receiver to lock onto its target. The 'Alpha' variant of the JSOW carries the same sub-munitions as the CBU-87, while the weaponry fitted into the 'Bravo' variant is identical to that used in the CBU-97.

Associated avionics and software improvements were also made during this stage of the upgrade cycle to allow the jet to convey these weapons.

Although the B-1B never carried nuclear cruise missiles, the AGM-158 JASSM conventional cruise missile can be launched at a stand-off range of 200 miles from the target. The weapon features a 1000-lb warhead.

Finally, as with the JDAM tail/strake kit, the WCMD is a tail assembly and FZU-39/B proximity sensor combination which is designed to improve the accuracy of the munitions by taking prevailing weather conditions into account when launched. The WCMD kit can be added to the CBU-87/89/97 weapons. These CBUs are designated -103, -104 and -105 when they are fitted with the WCMD. The WCMD munitions are placed on a Seventy-six

GBU-31 munitions are mounted on a CRL ready to be fitted into the Lancer's weapons bay (*Senior Airman Michael Keller*)

This spectacular photograph shows a B-1B from the 37th BS/28th BW at Ellsworth preparing for a night sortie. The shot betrays the aircraft's impressive wingspan (*28th BW*)

Enhanced Conventional Bomb Module which is in turn fitted into each of the 'Bone's' weapons bays. The B-1B can carry a total of 30 WCMDs, 12 JSOWs and 24 JASSMs.

The Block E upgrade, which was scheduled for completion in 2005, will allow the aircraft to carry a mix of these weapons, and to launch all of them simultaneously. This was proven on 2 May 2002 when a B-1B from the Global Power Bomber Combined Test Force, located at Edwards AFB, California, targeted three different weapons systems – in this case a single Mk 84, three Mk 82s and four CBU-89s – at three separate targets placed 10,000-ft apart during a single 20-second pass.

As well as adding to the targeting and tasking versatility of the B-1B, this capability has meant that a single jet can accomplish what would typically take three bombing passes, or a coordinated strike by three aircraft. By using this new capability, the USAF will be able to dramatically decrease the number of assets put in harm's way during future aircraft attacks.

The final stage of the CMUP (known as Block F) will see further improvements to the B-1B's defences, notably the AN/ALE-50 decoy. The programme was initiated in 2003, and it is scheduled to be completed by 2009, although the USAF cancelled the Defensive Systems Upgrade Program portion of the project. This would have included comprehensive improvements to the aircraft's DCS, with the ALQ-161 being replaced with the ALR-56M radar warning receiver and the US Navy-developed Integrated Defensive Electronic Countermeasures radio frequency jamming system, which includes a Fibre Optic Towed Decoy.

Part of the attraction for this DCS upgrade was that it would have reduced the number of defensive system 'boxes' in the aircraft from 120 to 34, thus saving approximately 4000 lbs in weight.

DESERT FOX AND NOBLE ANVIL

As history has shown, Operation *Desert Storm* (ODS), which ejected the Iraq Army from Kuwait in March 1991, was far from being the end of the United States' troubled relationship with the Iraqi President Saddam Hussein. The outcome, as the world saw in 2003, was Operation *Iraqi Freedom* (OIF), which finally removed Saddam from power. However, America's Iraqi journey from ODS to the capture of Saddam was punctuated with numerous spats and skirmishes as the US Air Force, Navy and Marine Corps, together with the RAF, sought to enforce the so-called No-Fly Zones over northern and southern Iraq during operations *Northern Watch* and *Southern Watch.* The largest of these skirmishes occurred in December 1998, and was codenamed Operation *Desert Fox* (ODF).

The B-1B had almost received its combat debut one month earlier during Operation *Desert Thunder.* From 1997, the Iraqi regime had shown itself to be increasingly unwilling to cooperate with United Nations' (UN) weapons inspectors. B-1B bombers armed with CBU-97 SFWs had already deployed to Bahrain once in 1997 when Saddam indulged in some 'sabre-rattling', although they were not used. *Desert Thunder* was in some ways a show of force – the 'big stick' which was brandished while negotiations between the UN and the Iraqi government were ongoing.

Once ODF got underway, *Desert Thunder* would become the term by which the military deployments for ODF would be known. B-1Bs would deploy to Oman from the 28th BW at Ellsworth and the 7th BW at Dyess as part of the 366th Air Expeditionary Wing (AEW).

By 15 November 1998, the first B-1Bs had arrived in Oman, although all of their support equipment was held in Europe for a week as last-minute diplomatic manoeuvring was played out to try and prevent any hostilities between the US-led Coalition and Iraq. On 30 November the 'Bones' began exhaustive flight training, although this was concluded on 15 December when the bomber crews were told that they would be flying operational missions the following day. They were told to take their sleeping pills and get their mandatory rest before the missions began.

Launched on 16 December, ODF was intended to punish Saddam and his regime for its refusal to comply with the demands of weapons inspectors from the United Nations' Special Commission (UNSCOM) to be able to inspect Iraqi presidential palaces for materials relating to Saddam's development of nuclear, biological or chemical Weapons of Mass Destruction (WMD). Yet it was entirely possible that the motivations for the attack were also to assist dissident elements of the

Iraqi Army, which were believed to be attempting to overthrow the Iraqi President. Saddam Hussein's sleeping quarters at the Al-Qaddissiya presidential compound at Radwaniyah, about nine miles west of central Baghdad, near Saddam International Airport, were targeted during ODF, along with buildings that housed elements of the Iraqi security apparatus such as the Special Security Organisation and the Special Republican Guard (SRG). Moreover, Saddam's presidential palace at Lake Tharthar was attacked with a salvo of BGM-109 Tomahawk sea-launched land-attack missiles following reports that the Iraqi leader was residing there.

Whether the underlying reasons for ODF were to topple Saddam, punish him for non-compliance with UN demands or to do both, an impressive number of targets were hit during the combat phase. In total, ODF saw 28 Surface-to-Air Missiles (SAMs) and Integrated Air Defence (IAD) facilities attacked, with one destroyed, 19 regime 'security facilities' attacked, with two destroyed, five airfields attacked but none destroyed, 11 weapons production facilities attacked, with none destroyed, 23 command and control facilities attacked, with five destroyed, and eight Republican Guard facilities attacked, with none destroyed. US Department of Defense (DoD) estimates talked of 1600 troops being killed during ODF, and Iraq's WMD capabilities being set back two years.

It has been reported that 250 targets were originally selected by the DoD for attack during ODF, although this was later reduced to approximately 100, as the US political leadership under President Bill Clinton did not want the strikes to continue beyond the start of the Muslim holy month of Ramadan. ODF was exceptional in being the first massed air offensive which saw the use of predominantly 'smart' munitions as opposed to 'dumb' ordnance. US air- and sea-launched cruise missiles also performed around two-thirds of the attacks.

ODF was to provide the Lancer with its combat debut. Brig Gen Michael McMahan, Commander of the 7th BW, remarked that 'everyone in the B-1B community knows the capability of this weapons system, and now we've been given the opportunity to show the world the powerful tools we bring to the fight'. A total of seven jets participated in ODF, all of which had undergone Block D of the CMUP prior to their involvement. This had enhanced the aircrafts' conventional capabilities by allowing them to target aim points using satellite-derived GPS coordinates, which significantly improved accuracy when compared with radar offset bombing.

The 7th and 28th BWs were able to demonstrate their abilities on 17 December – one day after the ODF air strikes had begun. A single Lancer from each wing (call-signs 'SLAM-01' and 'SLAM-02') flew from Sheikh Isa air base, in Bahrain, to attack a target near Baghdad. The use of two bombers in this strike was not unusual, given that B-1B crews had always trained to operate in 'two-ship' formations.

The targeting abilities of the B-1Bs were helped in no small part by an E-8C Joint Surveillance Target Attack Radar System (J-STARS) aircraft of the 12th Air Control Squadron flying from Prince Sultan air base, in Saudi Arabia, which provided both Lancers with real-time targeting information. The 76th Space Operations Squadron also

B-1B 86-0109 ***SPECTRE*** **of the 13th BS/7th BW prepares for its imminent deployment to the Middle East for ODF at Ellsworth AFB, the aircraft departing its home base with a full load of Mk 82 bombs in its Conventional Rotary Launcher (*USAF*)**

supplied satellite imagery for Lancer pre-strike mission planning and post-strike Bomb Damage Assessment (BDA). During ODF, over the course of four days, Lancers conducted three, two-aircraft sorties, dropping 500-lb Mk 82 gravity bombs on each occasion.

On 17 December, the two Lancer crews arrived in the Operations Room at 2230 hrs local time. Thirty minutes was spent studying the composition of the strike package that the bombers would fly with – in this case the two Lancers would be supported by two F-14 Tomcat fighters, one EA-6B Prowler Electronic Countermeasure/Suppression of Enemy Air Defence (ECM/SEAD) aircraft, six F/A-18 Hornet strike aircraft and two extra Hornets dedicated to SEAD operations. The Saudi Arabians would not permit offensive aircraft to be based on their soil, so all these supporting jets had to fly from aircraft carriers. The Saudis did, however, allow E-3C Airborne Warning And Control System (AWACS) aircraft to fly from their soil.

After a low-level flight along the same 'Blue Two' corridor which the bomber crews had practised flying in days before, the B-1B crews flew through the airspace of Bahrain, Oman and the United Arab Emirates, before arriving over the Persian Gulf. Here, they waited to team-up with their Navy escorts. The package then flew over Kuwait and headed for Tallil, in southern Iraq, before turning north for Baghdad.

At around this time, a Prowler fired an AGM-88 High-Speed Anti-Radiation Missile (HARM) at an SA-6 SAM battery which had been detected at Tallil. The aircraft flew towards Baghdad, before executing a feint and heading for Al Kut. The crews were flying the mission using NVGs, and they began to see AAA lighting up the target area as the bombers approached. Each B-1B carried its full load of Mk 82s, and a total of 120 weapons slammed into the barracks. One SA-2 was fired on the bombers as they neared the Iraq-Kuwait border on their return home, but no damage was done. The bombers arrived back at Sheikh Isa at around 0700 hrs after a six-hour sortie.

The mission had severely damaged the Al Nida Republican Guard division barracks at Al Kut, northwest of the Iraqi capital. The idea of

The results of a 'stick' of Mk 82 bombs dropped by B-1Bs' 'SLAM 01' and 'SLAM 02' on 17 December 1998. The strike devastated the Al Kut barracks, leaving many buildings severely damaged and others destroyed outright. The attack gave a foretaste of what the aircraft would be capable of in Kosovo four months later (*US Department of Defense*)

hitting the Republican Guard was to drive a wedge between them and the regular Iraqi Army, and to encourage the latter to rise against Saddam. 'Psyops' missions had dropped leaflets days before, informing regular Army units that they would not be deliberately targeted during the operation. The B-1B raid on Al Kut was seen as a pivotal part of this strategy. The lead aircraft performing the attack was 86-0096 from the 28th BS/7th BW, commanded by Lt Col Steve Wolborsky.

The Al Kut barracks were in the heart of the so-called Super Missile Engagement Zone (SuperMEZ) which ring-fenced Baghdad and the surrounding area. Despite Saddam's air defence systems being degraded in a piecemeal fashion since the establishment of the No-Fly Zones, Iraqi air defences were still considered to be extremely strong. Soviet-built SA-2, SA-3, SA-6 and SA-8 SAM systems were supplemented by ZSU-23-4 and S-60 AAA pieces.

During a press conference shortly after the Al Kut attack, Rear Adm Thomas R Wilson, vice director for intelligence for the US DoD Joint Chiefs of Staff, noted that the weapons used by the B-1B were not 'precision-guided ordnance. It was the old way, although it's hard to beat a lot of bombs sometimes. The pilot walked a stick of bombs across this barracks'. The other major target for the Lancer force during ODF was the oil refinery at Iraq's second city of Basra.

ODF was sufficient to give the Iraqi leader a bloody nose by degrading his WMD capabilities, yet the Lancers' business with Saddam Hussein's regime remained unfinished as the tyrant remained in power. The final battle would be fought during OIF four years later – a conflict in which the B-1B would play a pivotal role – but before then the 'Bones' would head for the Balkans.

85-0091 and 85-0083, both from the 77th 'War Eagles' BS prepare for a mission from Fairford during OAF. The AN/ALE-50 defensive system which was rapidly fitted to the aircraft to make them mission-capable for *Noble Anvil* was installed in the jets' rear tail fairing (*B-1B Systems Program Office*)

OPERATION *NOBLE ANVIL*

The 7th and 28th BWs at Dyess and Ellsworth would enjoy several months of respite from combat operation before getting involved in an altogether different conflict miles away, both in terms of geography and characteristics, from ODF. Despite the war in the Balkans having been officially ended by the Dayton Accords of

A B-1B from the 77th BS/28th BW sits on the ramp at Fairford in April 1999 with its weapons bay doors open. A total of nine Lancers deployed to the RAF base during *Noble Anvil*, the aircraft arriving with their support equipment, which was brought in by two C-5B Galaxies. One of the latter can just be seen behind this B-1B (*B-1 Systems Program Office*)

1995, Serbian President Slobodan Milosevic subsequently began a crackdown against the secessionist ambitions of the Kosovar Albanian population in the southern Yugoslav province of Kosovo.

In 1997, the Kosovo Liberation Army (KLA) had begun a guerrilla campaign directed at the Serbian presence in the province, notably against the Army and law enforcement authorities. Belgrade had responded by increasing its security posture, beginning with an offensive against the movement in the summer of 1998. This resulted in what was dubbed a campaign of 'ethnic cleansing' against the Kosovar population, which was being ejected from the province by the Serbian army and Special Police units.

Mindful of its failure to prevent genocide against the Bosnian Muslim population in the early 1990s, and after the failure of the Rambouillet talks of February 1999, which aimed to find a peaceful conclusion to the crisis, the United States, along with the North Atlantic Treaty Organisation (NATO) made the decision to begin a series of air strikes, codenamed Operation *Allied Force* (OAF), against the Serbian government, and its military presence in Kosovo. These were aimed at removing the latter from the province, and paving the way for the entry of a NATO-led force to restore the peace.

Supreme Allied Commander in Europe (SACEUR) Gen Wesley Clark left no doubt as to the Alliance's intentions;

'We're going to systematically and progressively attack, disrupt, degrade, devastate and ultimately, unless President Milosevic complies with the demands of the international community, we're going to destroy his forces and their facilities.'

The stage was set for a determined air campaign which would see the weight of ten NATO members, along with France, attempt to achieve exactly what had been spelt out by Gen Clark.

The B-1B would bring its range, payload and Low Observable (LO) characteristics to the fight. Initially, four B-1Bs, all of which had

A B-1B from the 77th BS/28th BW is marshalled onto the flightline at Fairford during *Noble Anvil* in April 1999 – the US contribution to OAF. Three other Lancers can be seen parked on the ramp in the background at the huge base (*B-1B Systems Program Office*)

undergone Block D of the CMUP, were deployed to their Forward Operating Location at RAF Fairford, in Gloucestershire. Only seven aircraft had so far undergone Block-D of the CMUP, which had also seen the aircraft installed with the software necessary for the delivery of the GPS-guided BLU-109B 2000-lb hard-target penetrator JDAM.

Lt Col David 'Gunny' Béen, CO of the 37th BS, flew Lancers during Operation *Noble Anvil* (ONA), and he argues that 'the jet came of age in *Allied Force*. It was our first opportunity for sustained operations, which we were able to demonstrate we could perform. It really justified the jet. That probably ensured that we stayed around for years to come'.

The CMUP upgrades installed in the B-1B over the previous five years were the primary reasons why the aircraft was able to play such a full role in this operation. The Block D upgrade was already in motion prior to OAF, although it was greatly accelerated to make a number of Block D Lancers available for operations. According to Col Anthony F Przybyslawski, CO of the 28th BW during OAF, 'we were most definitely in an accelerated effort that last week before the ONA deployment began. All the aircraft flight-testing the new systems were sent to the conflict'.

The first aircraft to receive the AN/ALE-50 towed decoy system upgrade had done so on 29 January, and the 28th BW was due to have seven such aircraft available by April 1999.

While the testing and evaluation of the Block D aircraft was underway, the call for the Lancers to participate in OAF came from ACC on 26 March. For all intents and purposes, Ellsworth's Lancers were ready to participate, save for a block cycle 'update' which saw new software installed into the aircrafts' defensive systems to allow them to correctly identify and counter enemy radar. The latter were presumably systems such as the 1S91 'Straight Flush' and RSN-125 'Low Blow' air-defence radars which were being used by the Serbian Air Defence Force. The updates, which would normally take several months to install, were completed in 100 hours.

The 53rd Test and Evaluation Group (TEG) at Eglin AFB, in Florida, was responsible for carrying out the block cycle 'update', with new mission and data software having been written by military and civilian test engineers from the 36th Engineering and Test Squadron (ETS). The latter began to test the new software on 27 March, laboratory work was completed by the 29th and flight testing was concluded 24 hours later!

Lt Col Lou Martucci, Operations Officer at the 36th ETS, remembered that 'to meet the dates they wanted it, the electronic warfare mission data had to be done very quickly'. However, the 36th

ETS did not achieve this feat on its own, with technicians from the 16th, 28th and 68th Test Squadrons also assisting. As soon as the update had been completed, the second detachment from the 53rd TEG flew a solitary modified B-1B to the Eglin land and water test facility – home of the 46th Test Wing – to check that the new systems operated correctly on the jet. Flight test time usually has to be booked weeks in advance at the range, but Lt Col Gregg Bourke, Integrated Systems Flight Commander for the 36th ETS, recalls that the '46th Test Wing allowed us to get on the range as soon as we needed it'.

Despite the Block-D upgrade, it would not be the Lancer's ability to deliver GPS-guided munitions during the conflict which would be exploited. Post-war, it was reported that B-1Bs principally expended Mk 82 'dumb' bombs during ONA.

At the start of the conflict, there had been some discussions over whether to fly the B-1Bs directly from Ellsworth AFB to their targets in Serbia and Kosovo, or whether to base the aircraft in Europe for their missions. 509th BW B-2A stealth bombers were already flying missions from their home at Whiteman AFB, Missouri, and Col Przybyslawski noted that 'there was a discussion (in ACC) during the build-up about flying sorties from Ellsworth. Finally, a decision came out of USAFE (USAF Europe) to just go over there'. This was no doubt because flying from the CONUS would have resulted in missions of up to 30 hours in duration – far in excess of the seven-hour mission times which could be gained from flying from Fairford.

By 29 March, five Lancers from the 77th BS, along with one spare

The Lancer was included in the OAF airpower 'mix' due to its overwhelming bomb-carrying capability. The Mk 82 500-lb 'slick' was the weapon of choice for the 'Bone' in *Noble Anvil*. Here, a weapons loader gingerly moves the munitions from a bomb trolley to a nearby Conventional Rotary Launcher. It was ordnance like this which was responsible for devastating Serbian area targets (*B-1B Systems Program Office*)

Easy does it! Mk 82s are loaded onto the rotary launcher in one of the B-1B's weapons bays. At the time of OAF, the USAF was in the early stages of transforming the Lancer into a near-precision conventional attack aircraft. However, during *Noble Anvil* the B-1B was more of an old-fashioned 'bomb truck', bringing brute force to bear, while its B-2A Spirit cousin conducted surgical strikes (*B-1B Systems Program Office*)

The pilot and co-pilot of a Fairford-based B-1B read through their jet's maintenance paperwork prior to performing their preflight walkaround checks at ramp level (*USAF*)

aircraft from the 37th BS and two C-5B Galaxy freighters carrying support personnel and equipment, had departed from Ellsworth bound for Fairford. All of the aircraft had arrived in the UK and were ready for operations by 1 April, and all the Lancers were under the command of the 100th AEW.

In total, nine Lancers participated in ONA. The first five to arrive at Fairford were 85-0075 (then with the 77th BS and now with the 419th Flight Test Squadron at Edwards AFB), 85-0083 from the 34th BS, 85-0091 from the 77th BS, 86-0102 from the 37th BS and 85-0073 from the 13th BS. Once operations were underway, the B-1Bs would be rotated through Fairford, with 85-0075 leaving on 11 April, 85-0073 departing 15 days later, 85-0083 departing on

Below
Lancer 85-0075 of the 77th BS sits under a partially cloudy Gloucestershire sky whilst being readied for another mission to Serbia. This aircraft left Fairford a mere 11 days after its arrival. The jet's early departure, in contrast with some of the other aircraft deployed, may have been due to mechanical problems (*B-1B Program Office*)

Bottom
'Bone' 86-0097 of the 77th BS/28th BW prepares to land on Fairford's runway 09/27 to signal the end of another marathon mission to the Balkans. This aircraft spent a month at the base before returning home to Ellsworth towards the end of the campaign (*B-1B Systems Program Office*)

29 May and 85-0091 leaving on 24 June. Other jets to deploy to Fairford included the 13th BS's 85-0074, which stayed in the UK from 8 April until 6 June, and 86-0097, which arrived on 24 April and returned to the CONUS on 24 June. 86-0129 and 86-0104, from the 34th and 37th BSs respectively, arrived on 15 May and 3 June and left on 25 and 24 June. All nine B-1Bs had departed by 26 June.

There was always a minimum number of four active jets, along with a spare (usually a Block C B-1B), at Fairford throughout ONA, although this would sometimes increase to six when aircraft were being swapped over. This usually resulted in six Lancers being at Fairford for between three and four days. From 30 May, the number of B-1Bs at Fairford declined to four aircraft, and this remained constant until 25 June, when only a solitary jet was left.

The two reserve aircraft – 86-0102 from the 37th BS and 86-0129 from the 34th BS – stayed at Fairford for 42 and 48 days respectively. It has been reported that the most capable jets (i.e. those which had suffered the fewest engineering problems) were the aircraft which remained at Fairford for the longest periods during ONA. B-1B 85-0091 spent more than 80 days at the base, while 85-0074, 85-0083 and 86-0097 remained at Fairford for around 60 days.

During the 78-day air war, each 77th BS aircraft performed a total of 25 sorties. Lt Col Béen remembers that for the B-1B crews 'we only had four Block D jets flying out of Fairford, so we were not totally rushed off our feet. We were living the "rock star" lifestyle. We landed when the sun came up and we slept during the day. We were flying every other day'.

The first B-1B mission occurred on 2 April against the Novi Sud petroleum production facility at Pancevo, northeast of Belgrade. Although ONA was originally limited to only 'tactical' targets at the start of the campaign, it became clear that hitting such sites alone would not persuade President Milosevic to fold. Instead, the target set was expanded to cover 'strategic' installations such as the Novi Sud facility, which was literally helping to oil the Serbian war machine.

This target could only be destroyed by area bombing, and the Lancer, with its small RCS, was the ideal aircraft for the job. In many ways Novi Sud was also an ideal target, spread over a big area, and presenting a large radar signature. The combined load of 168 Mk 82 'slicks' dropped from the two bombers that were sortied had no trouble knocking out the key sections of the plant.

85-0083 of the 34th BS/28th BW spent 60 days at Fairford, proving to be one of the most reliable aircraft of the *Noble Anvil* campaign (*B-1B Systems Program Office*)

These Mk 82 bombs are lined up on an ammunition-handling truck, waiting to be loaded into the weapons bay of the 77th BS Lancer parked in the background. The access ladder in the crew compartment is down and the aircraft awaits the arrival of the four-man team who will fly the bomber over western Europe and the Adriatic Sea and then onto its targets in Serbia and Kosovo (*B-1B Systems Program Office*)

However, after the bomb run, the weapons bay doors on one of the B-1Bs failed to close. The Lancer was subsequently targeted by a Serbian SAM, although a combination of defensive manoeuvres, chaff and electronic countermeasures defeated the missile. The weapon succeeded in forcing the bomber into the engagement zone of a second SAM, however, which the crew was also able to defeat.

According to the pilot of the aircraft, Capt Gerald Goodfellow, at the first indication of a SAM launch 'your training kicks in. It feels very natural. You don't really think about it until later on, when the mission is completed. You take on an almost business-like attitude. You have to beat that missile. When I'm up there, my biggest worry isn't about getting shot down, but about missing the target. As a whole, the crew is concentrating as one putting those bombs on target'.

The open weapons bay doors and the manoeuvring of the aircraft caused Goodfellow's Lancer to use more fuel than anticipated, leaving the bomber with insufficient fuel to return to Fairford. During the mission, the B-1B was also struck by lightning, which blew off a section of the aircraft's horizontal stabiliser, but the crew was still able to get the aircraft home. Goodfellow remembered that 'we felt a huge relief at the completion of the mission. The SAMs came closer than we'd anticipated, and after thinking about it for a couple of days, we were glad to have survived'.

Retired Air Force Chief of Staff Gen John Jumper was Commander USAFE and Commander Allied Air Forces Central Europe during OAF, and he remembers clearly how well the AN/ALE-50 towed decoy worked on this first mission;

Ellsworth-based 77th BS B-1B 86-0097 departs Fairford on 28 April 1999, Balkans-bound. The aircraft's bomb load, and the relatively short flight time from Fairford, meant that the small B-1B force played a valuable role in keeping the pressure on Belgrade (*USAF*)

If President Milosevic had ever needed proof that NATO was determined to see *Allied Force* through to the bitter end, then the presence of the Bone at Fairford must have helped with the arm-twisting. Three Lancers, all from the 77th BS, with 85-0075 in the foreground, are parked on the flightline, awaiting tasking. The impact of the B-1B on the war vastly outweighed the small numbers which were deployed (*B-1B Systems Program Office*)

'The pair of B-1Bs came down south over the Adriatic Sea in formation with their ALE-50 towed decoys deployed, and we watched the radars in Montenegro track the bombers as they turned the corner around Macedonia and headed up into Kosovo. We watched the radars, in real time, hand off the targets to the SA-6s, which came up in full-target track and fired their missiles. Those missiles took the ALE-50s off the back end of the B-1s just like they were designed to do. The B-1s went on and hit their targets.'

Lt Col Béen remembers that 'the B-1Bs' countermeasures was a major argument for the aircraft going into the Balkans theatre. Gen Jumper wanted it because of the towed decoy system, and it proved to be very effective against the Serbian threat'.

The Lancer's Defensive Avionics System (DAS) provided some headaches for the maintenance crews back at Fairford, however. According to B-1B commander Maj Gary Backes, the threat level to the bombers was 'more aggressive than we had anticipated. There were quite a few sorties that were "right in their face". But with SEAD and the defensive systems, we were very comfortable. Our major problem was, quite frankly, the DAS. For the first week-and-a-half we were consuming a lot of DAS line replacement units. That happened with the new bombers we brought in later as well'.

At the beginning of the conflict the B-1Bs would be flying in strike packages of two Lancers, plus two B-52H Stratofortresses, all of which

A 77th BS B-1B returns to Fairford towards the end of the campaign. In the foreground is a 2nd BW B-52H, which boasts an impressive mission tally comprised exclusively of AGM-86C CALCM silhouettes. Eight 'Buffs' were deployed to Fairford from Barksdale AFB, Louisiana, for OAF (*USAF*)

A CBU-97 SFW is prepared for transfer to a weapons truck before being loaded into a Lancer. The use of cluster munitions proved controversial in the Balkans because of the high volume of 'duds' – unexploded submunitions which littered the battlefield. Indeed, it is believed that none were actually dropped from a B-1B during OAF (*B-1B Systems Program Office*)

would deploy Mk 82 bombs. One of the reasons why the Lancers were dropping this weapon exclusively against area targets could have been because of a shortage of JDAM. The latter were primarily set aside for B-2As, which were operating from the CONUS, although the Lancers were thought to have possibly dropped some JDAM too. However, a B-1B crewman commented post-war that the Lancers did not drop a single J-weapon during the entire conflict. 'We did not take the JDAM capability with us. Mk 82s were all we dropped'.

One report commented that the 'B-1Bs were asked early on to go after those targets that required not precision, but brute force'. In one instance, cluster munitions (notably CBU-87s) were fitted to a Lancer Conventional Bomb Module, but they were never used.

Despite problems with the DAS, the Lancer's offensive avionics such as the SAR gave the B-1B crews good situational awareness even when the weather began to take a turn for the worse over Kosovo during the first 45 days of the air war. Maj Backes argued that 'probably the strongest suit we had was the SAR, especially as we got closer to the CAS role. We could target any metal in the target area very accurately'.

The SAR/Mk 82 bomb combination was especially efficient for the aircraft. Col Przybyslawski noted that 'sometimes, the radar and the "dumb" bombs were more accurate than the precision weapons. When the Serbs thought they had cloud deck over their heads, we changed their minds'.

Yet despite the effectiveness of the SAR, ONA was characterised by tight rules of engagement regarding the conditions under which

Lancer 85-0075 from the 77th BS/28th BW quickly gets airborne with a little help from the afterburners on a rainy day in western England. During OAF, television audiences around the world got used to seeing the Lancer's dramatic take-offs from Fairford, along with the more ponderous efforts of the B-52H (*B-1B Systems Program Office*)

ordnance could be deployed. Considerations over collateral damage and aircrew casualties dominated NATO planning. Maj Backes recalled that 'there were very specific requirements in the spin about cloud cover in the AOR. In some cases we were a little frustrated because it seemed a little too restrictive. The general rule was when in doubt come home'.

The bombers were equipped with the Multi-Source Tactical System (MSTS) computer which received and processed signals intelligence, electronics intelligence and reconnaissance imagery in real-time from four Ultra High Frequency satellite channels. This allowed targeting data to be passed from several sources, including the Combined Air Operations Centre (CAOC) at Vicenza, in Italy, directly into the B-1B cockpit. The MSTS could display new information regarding the electronic order of battle and targeting imagery.

The equipment was highly valued given that the bombers were directed on several occasions to change targets during missions. This would set precedence for Lancer tasking in Afghanistan and Iraq, and was of great benefit towards the end of the conflict when B-1B missions were flown in 'terminal guidance' mode. The latter would see formations of two Lancers fly into Serbian airspace and then receive targeting information from the CAOC via the MSTS.

Lt Col Béen remembered that 'this was a new concept for us at the time, working with Forward Air Controllers (FACs) who would direct us onto the targets. Gen Jumper asked if we could do this, and we had been practising these missions to a lesser extent in the B-1 community for years. We got our targets en route, and we received an experimental version of the MSTS that featured a moving map and a way to receive secure e-mails with targeting data. It gave us threat data, targeting data and imagery. We could then compare what was on the SAR picture with the imagery that was sent to us'.

In the final analysis, the B-1B made a considerable contribution to ONA. The aircraft flew 74 combat sorties over Serbia, and during the campaign released a total of 5000 Mk 82 'dumb' bombs. The effectiveness of the Lancer during OAF is beyond doubt. One report commented that its participation 'was a major milestone for the bomber once widely believed to be a "hanger queen" that would never see combat'.

The availability of the aircraft was also impressive. Despite the Lancer being characterised as a bomber which suffered from technical glitches, Lt Col Charles H 'Chuck' McGuirk, deputy Operations Group Command Forward during OAF, said 'I can tell you that 90 per cent of the time we could have launched all four (Block-D) jets'.

According to Lancer pilots such as Maj Backes, the handling of the bomber, which was said have the manoeuvrability of a fighter, was also validated in the conflict;

'My respect for the B-1B went up immediately. You were always able to drag it to the target. When I called on the jet to get out the way because something was in the air, it always did. If I needed extra speed or altitude it was always there. That made the crews more confident in the later phases of the campaign, when defences that in theory would have been destroyed in the first three days were still a threat.'

ENDURING FREEDOM

At the beginning of OEF, the US airbase at Diego Garcia was home to all the Lancers committed to the war – this jet is seen departing the island base in late 2001. However, this was changed soon after the campaign had commenced to include Thumrait, in Oman, so as to allow the aircraft to be closer to the theatre in order to generate more sorties. This made a huge difference to the troops on the ground in-theatre. The importance of the conflicts in Afghanistan and Iraq to the B-1B, and vice versa, were recently detailed by Robert Butler, Lancer site manager at Dyess AFB;

'There were a couple of years in the early 1990s where it looked like the B-1B force might be cancelled altogether. Since its role in *Desert Fox*, however, the bomber has been the weapon of choice. Battlefield commanders ask for that weapon above anything else because of the virtual "delicatessen" of the weapon bays, and the precision weapons we can load into them' (*USAF*)

'The United States' national security depends on long-range bomber capability. Our mission, not unlike any other bomb squadron in the Combat Air Forces, is to guarantee America's freedom – and that's why we're here.'

These words were prophetically spoken by Lt Col Jeffrey Smith, CO of the 37th BS, in February 2000, some 17 months before the terrorist attacks in New York and Washington DC on 11 September 2001. They perfectly describe the role that the B-1B Lancer would play in this hit-and-run conflict against the Taleban student militia, and their al-Qaeda associates (collectively known as al-Qaeda/Taleban, or 'AQT'), in the mountains and plains of Afghanistan.

A total of eight B-1Bs were deployed by the 28th BW as part of the 28th AEW to Diego Garcia, in the Indian Ocean, prior to the wing redeploying to Thumrait AFB, in Oman, in mid-December 2001. From 1 January 2002, the bombers operated in Oman under the control of the 405th AEW.

The first Lancer to fly in combat was 86-0123 from the 9th BS/7th BW, christened *"LET'S ROLL"* after the comment made by Todd Beamer, who was a passenger aboard United Airlines Flight 93 which was one of the four airliners hijacked by al-Qaeda terrorists on 11 September 2001. Although the Boeing 757 crashed with the loss of all onboard, the actions of Todd Beamer and several other passengers who overpowered the hijackers is thought to have averted a fourth attack, possibly on the Camp David Presidential residence in Maryland.

A B-52H from the 28th AEW takes off from Diego Garcia at the start of a marathon combat mission on 22 October 2001 in support of OEF. Parked on the ramp in the foreground, opposite a row of KC-10As, are six B-1Bs from the 28th BW and a solitary MO-coded jet from the 34th BS. B-1Bs, B-2As and B-52Hs expended more than 80 per cent of the bomb tonnage dropped on combat missions over Afghanistan in the first ten days of OEF. Targets hit included early-warning radars, ground forces, command-and-control facilities, al-Qaeda infrastructure, airfields and aircraft (*SSgt Shane Cuomo*)

One of the first units from the 28th BW to deploy to Diego Garcia was the 34th BS from Ellsworth AFB. This unit was eventually joined in the 405th AEW by the 9th, 13th and 28th BSs, all from Dyess AFB. The 28th BW's 77th BS also deployed, as did the 128th BS of the 116th BW, formerly of Robins AFB, Georgia – the latter wing converted to E-8C J-STARS in September 2002. This switch followed the mid-2001 decision announced by Secretary of State for Defense Donald H Rumsfeld to delete the 116th BS Lancers from the inventory as part of a plan to remove a total of 32 B-1Bs from active service on the grounds of cost.

Summing up the mood of the 7th BW prior to its deployment to the Indian Ocean, the unit's vice-commander, Col Thomas Bell, announced that 'the men and women of Dyess Air Force Base did not ask for this war, but they are fully prepared and ready to conduct the mission'. Lt Col 'Joe', a B-1B pilot with the 7th BW, summarised his own feelings when he stated at the time that 'many of the Dyess airmen who out-processed at the Deployment Control Center were glad they were able to help. Ever since the 11 September events happened, I've been anxious to do my part'.

Lt Col 'Joe', his colleagues, the weapons and the aircraft would indeed play their part in OEF. The Lancers, along with the venerable B-52H Stratofortress, flew ten per cent of the strike missions and delivered 11,500 weapons during the major combat phase of OEF from the commencement of operations on 7 October 2001 through to the fall of Kandahar (the spiritual home of the Taleban), in southwest Afghanistan, exactly two months later. In fact, the Lancer expended more weapons on Afghanistan than any other aircraft during this phase, dropping nearly 40 per cent of all ordnance employed while flying five per cent of the strike sorties.

Capt Michael Fessler, who flew missions in OEF, recalled that the B-1B was 'used in Afghanistan for "on-call" firepower, and a lot of it. We were never really specifically assigned to CAS missions. One day you could be up there and be in a situation where you've got guys on the ground, whether they are US or Coalition troops, and they would call you up to perform a CAS mission for them'.

B-1B 86-0135 from the 9th BS/7th BW prepares to depart on a mission in support of OEF from Thumrait. Lt Gen James Light Jr, who was the commander of the Fifteenth Air Force when the Lancer first entered service in 1980s, spoke prophetically when he stated that the Lancer would 'remain an effective weapon system well into the 21st century' soon after its arrival at Dyess AFB. The first major conflict of the new millennium proved the General correct (*USAF*)

The B-1B played two major roles during OEF – smashing the Taleban's moribund command and control installations and its air force of rusting MiGs and Sukhois, and then providing CAS to US and Coalition troops as they began the war on the ground against AQT forces. Long-range bombers were a valuable asset during the campaign, as their fuel payloads enabled them to loiter over the battlefield for a longer period than carrier-based strike aircraft, and to fly the long ferry ranges from Diego Garcia and Thumrait to Afghanistan. They could also carry more weapons, including precision munitions, than tactical strike aircraft.

These attributes were praised post-war by Maj Gen Walter E Buchanan III, Deputy Chief-of-Staff for air and space operations at the Pentagon, who said that 'the bomber brings lots of muscle to the fight because of its long loiter time above the target area and high payload. So now we're talking about 24 JDAM or more, as opposed to fighters going in with, at best, typically four JDAM and not nearly as much loiter time'.

It was this tactical use of the bomber, which would have the desired strategic effect on the ground, that decimated the AQT and persuaded those that remained that their current adversary could not have been more different from the ill-equipped and often demoralised Soviet forces which their fore fathers had helped evict from Afghan soil some 12 years earlier.

Maj Gen Daniel P Leaf, director of operational requirements for air and space operations at the Pentagon, argues that 'at some point in the conflict the massed JDAM employment by the B-1Bs is when the Taleban and al-Qaeda leadership thought to themselves "this is a different, extraordinarily

Two of the three B-1Bs seen here are idling in the scorching Omani sun, their crews awaiting clearance to taxi out to Thumrait's vast runway (*USAF*)

A weapons loader at Diego Garcia prepares GBU-31 JDAM for a sortie. The OEF weapons combination of the Lancer and the JDAM got Taleban and al-Qaeda fighters out of their caves and on the run, leaving them vulnerable to be smacked hard by the accompanying B-52Hs flying CAS missions overhead. The Lancer's reputation soon spread amongst enemy ranks, as 9th BS 'Whizzo' Capt Jason Register recalled. 'On one mission, we got a call from a squad of Marines that was pinned down in a valley by enemy fire. We played a leading part in saving our guys that day, for although we didn't drop any bombs, our arrival on-scene gave the enemy something to think about, and they soon disengaged' (*USAF*)

more capable enemy. This realisation played a very big part in the routing of the Taleban and al-Qaeda'.

This unique conflict provided enduring images of US Special Operations Forces (SOF) Tactical Air Controllers (TACs) on horseback, riding side-by-side with their Northern Alliance anti-Taleban Afghan comrades, as they directed precision air strikes against AQT positions. Maj Gen Leaf noted the contribution of the Lancer to this image of hi-tech weaponry fighting in harsh terrain;

'The picture that is etched into my mind about the B-1B is the picture of an Afghan mountainside and a string of GBU-31 JDAM marching down a trench line.'

Such missions were a far cry from the low-level nuclear strike role that the Lancer was originally designed for.

Maj Gen Leaf also stated that 'if you had offered me the B-1B with JDAM in direct support of ground forces as a solution ten years ago, I would have laughed heartily because it's not what we envisioned. However, faced with a shift in what we have to do, we adjusted and used the aeroplane in an extraordinarily flexible manner over Afghanistan'.

This statement fits in with a wider change within the USAF about how weapons and aircraft are employed, with the emphasis swinging away from the 'platform' (i.e. the aircraft) to the capability – the task which the aircraft and its weapons have to achieve. Maj Gen Leaf again;

'When you're able to precisely drop a series of weapons like that,

While the Lancer is configured to carry 24 JDAMs, 16 weapons was a typical loadout for the bomber when performing missions in Afghanistan. This meant that part of the weapons bay was free to house an auxiliary fuel tank to increase the aircraft's range (*Capt James Conley*)

then that is really something. It's truly transformational in a combat sense.'

In one textbook Lancer attack, on 3 January 2002, four B-1Bs, together with four F/A-18 Hornets and an AC-130 gunship, devastated a large al-Qaeda cave complex at Zhawar Kili, in eastern Afghanistan. The installation was known to be a training camp, as well as an al-Qaeda regrouping, storage and sanctuary area. This was the same complex which had been struck by American cruise missiles in 1998 in retaliation for the terrorist bombings of the US Embassies in Kenya and Tanzania.

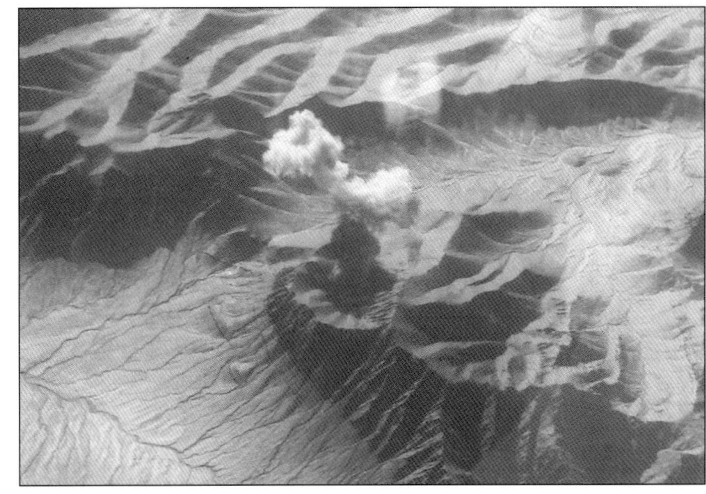

This photograph was taken from the cockpit of 77th BS/28th BW B-1B 86-0125 whilst the jet was over Afghanistan. It shows JDAM smashing into a cave complex during a CAS operation over the country in the summer of 2003 (*Capt Richard Morrison*)

The TAC, Lancer and JDAM combination was a potent mix. Not only did it enable pin-point and devastating attacks against AQT, but it also shortened the all-important 'sensor-to-shooter' cycle – the time taken between identifying a target by electronic or human means and striking it. Maj Gen Buchanan used an interesting analogy to explain just how advanced the battlespace was becoming in OEF thanks to this combination;

'When you take a look at the conditions on the ground that those young troops are going through, it's pretty amazing. We couldn't do it without them. For *Star Wars* fans, it reminds me of storm troopers, and what they envisioned the battlefield to look like. They are like Luke Skywalker on the ground using laser goggles and talking to fighters in space. If we have a way to identify a target, we can hit it. This allows us to have bombers doing close-air support and interdiction that they would never have been able to do in the past. The use of the bomber in the global war on terrorism is critical. If a terrorist cell is identified somewhere, in a matter of hours we can have an aircraft overhead with a JDAM precision weapon onboard that can reach out and touch them. This precision allows the United States to manage collateral damage. And from 40,000 ft! They'll never even know what happened until the bomb explodes.'

Lancers have also undergone some significant modifications to enable them to target AQT even more surgically as OEF has progressed. One addition includes a laptop computer for the mission commander and the pilot which enables them to see the offensive and defensive situations which are presented to the 'Whizzos' in the rear of the crew compartment.

JDAM are loaded onto a B-1B in preparation for a sortie from Diego Garcia. Not only did JDAM help the Lancers to become more surgical in their striking ability, it also enabled the USAF to reduce collateral damage, which was an important aspect of OEF (*USAF*)

Three of the major USAF platforms of OEF sit side-by-side on the Thumrait ramp. The Lancer in the foreground is parked next to E-3C AWACS aircraft and KC-135 tankers. AWACS would hand off targets to the B-1Bs, while the refuellers kept the aircraft airborne on-station, doing their job (*B-1B Systems Program Office*)

Capt Joe Delgado of the 7th Equipment Maintenance Squadron explained that 'this modification in particular has made the B-1B more effective in targeting hostile forces, while having more precision to avoid targeting friendly forces. The modification offers a "bird's eye" visual depiction of the battlespace with GPS accuracy. This allows for enhanced situational awareness for the crew members'.

The laptop computer idea was the brainchild of Col William Redmond, vice-commander of the 7th BW. Capt Steve Sturm, a weapons officer from the 7th Operations Support Squadron, noted that 'there have been plans in place to introduce this modification to the Air Force's B-1B fleet for years. Col Redmond felt the time was right to introduce the Dyess B-1Bs to this great modification since we were about to deploy. The old system got the job done, but it was like being in a NASCAR race with a horse and buggy. It just wasn't 21st century equipment'.

The B-1B wing had to initially maintain a 24-hour commitment to operations in OEF. Each mission shift would begin after 12 hours of mandatory crew rest before the sorties were flown. The mission 'show time' – when the crews report to the briefing – could begin at any time of the day, and was based primarily on the tactical situation on the battlefield.

Capt Fessler remembers that 'the time we would go on-station would vary day-to-day depending on what was going on, especially if you had other platforms in-theatre that were providing support. The days turned out to be really long. First of all, we had 24/7 operations, so there was really no downtime. You could be going on a mission anytime between 0800 hrs, 1200 hrs, 1600 hrs or 0200 hrs. You knew that you could be scheduled to fly at any of those times. You had to have had 12 hours of rest, and that was a set rule. You were required to have had that rest prior to the flight commencing'.

The first priority, according to Lt Col Dave Garrett, assistant

Suited-up and ready to go, a B-1B crew discuss final preparations with a member of the groundcrew whilst looking through their jet's paperwork. In the background, a Lancer from the 28th BW has just had its cockpit glazing cleaned (*B-1B Systems Program Office*)

B-1B crews soon got to know Afghanistan as a land of contrast, from the plains of the north to the mountainous central regions and the lush green hues of the western area. This photograph was taken in the summer of 2003 from the cockpit of 86-0125 (*Capt Richard Morrison*)

director of operations for the 37th Expeditionary Bomb Squadron (EBS), was to get something to eat. 'Hopefully after some good sleep, the chow hall was open for a meal before we took the crew bus to the operations building'. The crew then collected their life-support equipment. This included helmets, radios, handguns, survival vests and ejection seat harnesses. Lt Col Garrett noted that the personal radio, which included a built-in GPS, was vital. 'With GPS, if you ended up ejecting from the aircraft, satellites and rescue aircraft could identify who you were and where you were without even talking to you'.

Fed, watered and equipped, the crew moved to the Mission Briefing room to hear details about the sortie which they would be executing. 'We would go over the threat in certain areas and basically they'd give us all the information that we'd need to fly, which could take a few hours. It could be quicker, but they made an extra effort to ensure that we were fully briefed up', remembers Capt Fessler.

Typically, the proceedings in the Mission Briefing room would begin with a sermon. Capt Joseph Watson, who is a Chaplain from the 40th Air Expeditionary Group, explained that he 'either told a story or read a scripture passage which related to God's protection, help or battle against evildoers. The purpose of this was primarily to encourage and give confidence in God's protection and guidance on the mission. I always closed with a prayer asking for the safety and success of the mission'.

Boxes of chaff and flares are offloaded onto the ramp in preparation for loading into the expendables dispensers fitted into the B-1Bs parked on the Thumrait ramp. The Lancer has eight dispensers – four on each side of the bomber's centreline, recessed into the top of the fuselage above the forward weapons bay. Each can be loaded with either 120 chaff cartridges to screen the B-1B from enemy radar or 12 flares to decoy infrared-homing missiles. Once fired by the DSO, each payload follows a trajectory which is initially upward and to one side. The blooming chaff cloud instantly decelerates so as to pass directly aft of the jet, but the flares arch up and away from the aircraft's track (*USAF*)

Following the prayers, it was time for a weather and intelligence briefing. The latter focused on the tactical situation on the ground, noting any potential surface-to-air threats. Life-support was also highlighted, with the crew being told what would happen in the event of an emergency. Lt Col Garrett noted that 'they also briefed our survival and recovery plan should we end up on the ground in a survival situation'. Other points covered during the briefing included details on air refuelling, communications procedures and rules for entering and exiting the area of responsibility in which the aircraft would operate.

GBU-31 JDAM was the weapon of choice for the average B-1B mission, 37th BS 'Whizzo' Capt Patrick 'Pikey' McMahon recalling that 'we would usually only carry 16 JDAM, and we'd also have a fuel tank in the weapons bay'.

After the briefing, the crew visited the Aviation Resource Manager, who reviewed their flight plans and dealt with any last-minute changes which may have arisen. After this, the crew put on their flight suits and proceeded to their aircraft. On the ramp, they were met by the jet's crew chief, who delivered a quick briefing on the current status of the bomber. Prior to the aircrew's arrival, ground staff had typically spent up to five hours preparing the bomber for the mission. The aircrew then had around 90 minutes before departure.

Just to get the aircraft into a mission-capable state on the ramp was a challenge in itself according to SSgt Craig Kossow of the 40th Expeditionary Maintenance Squadron. 'The inspections, maintenance, and the paperwork require a coordinated effort by everyone on the flightline in order to get a jet ready to fly'. What followed in the cockpit was a series of checks to ensure that the B-1B was ready for combat. It was then time for the aircraft to taxi to the runway.

Capt McMahon summed up the average OEF Lancer sortie during this early war period. 'We'd take-off, meet a tanker around three hours into the flight, travel up a couple more hours into Afghanistan, receive directions from the CAOC, look at the radar and then wait for somebody to call us so that we could come in and do our thing. With our bombs gone, we would head for home after refuelling from a tanker. There was almost always a B-1B in-country'.

The flights to and from Afghanistan could take hours, but the crew were anything but idle during this time. Lt Col Garrett explained that

86-0125 *SWIFT JUSTICE* of the 34th BS sits on the ramp at Diego Garcia in late 2001 (*Capt Richard Morrison*)

'as we entered our operating area, we would communicate with numerous agencies, some of which were hundreds of miles away. Most importantly, we'd configure our aircraft to release weapons, including chaff and flares for self-defence'.

Once over the Afghan theatre, Lancers could spend up to five hours orbiting and waiting for a call to provide support. The crews would establish contact with a TAC during the on-call period and wait for a request to provide CAS. The TACs, who might have already been embroiled in an engagement in difficult conditions, impressed the B-1B crews with their controlling abilities. 'When they called, they were typically in a direct firefight with the enemy, most of the time on foot, in mountainous terrain ranging between 5000 ft and 10,000 ft', Lt Col Garrett recalled.

Capt Fessler remarked that 'you might have had guys that were on the ground near a weapons bunker or a cave which the anti-Coalition militia had been using as a refuge or for storage, and they'd call us in and we'd bomb that'.

Despite being high above the battle, the Lancer crews could often hear the ferocity of the fight raging below them through their headphones. Capt James Conley remembered one such mission;

'As we went in-country our troops came under fire, and once they came under fire they called us in to basically neutralise the threat. So we ended up doing our CAS role and dropped four GBU-31s into the area. After we dropped the second set, the inbound fires stopped, and the relief you could hear on ground guy's voice was significant. You could tell that we'd done what we were supposed to be doing.'

Lt Col Garrett explained that 'while in radio contact you would hear machine gun fire and guys yelling and breathing hard as they chase the enemy. It was amazing what they do. Our job was to be immediately available for (them) and if called, drop bombs on the enemy, who were often in very close proximity to the friendly forces'.

Capt Conley remembers that 'one night we were out there doing our standard flight when, about an hour-and-a-half into our on-call period, we received a message on the radio from the CAOC asking us to support a rescue mission. Some UN people had got caught up in a firefight between two militia groups in central Afghanistan, and they didn't have any air support apart from us. They had a Marine Corps rescue team which was flown in aboard several Black Hawks, and we were doing our combat air patrolling. Basically, we were searching for enemies, and we were also the standby jet if something happened, as they could call us in to drop weapons. So we were watching the rescue and we saw these helicopters approach on the radar and rescue them. We subsequently followed the H-60s until they got back safety'.

The Lancers were not just tasked with providing CAS. Indeed, they performed some rather unorthodox roles in comparison to the tasks that the bomber was first designed for. Convoys of US and Coalition troops would sometimes be escorted by B-1Bs providing airborne armed reconnaissance for the route ahead. Occasionally, ordnance would not be required, and instead the Lancer crew would be requested to perform a low-altitude, high-speed pass over enemy troops. This could have an important effect on the battlefield, as Lt

The pilot's instruments reveal the high speeds which the B-1B is easily capable of, flying straight and level over Afghanistan (*Capt Richard Morrison*)

Col Garrett explained. 'The low-altitude pass let the enemy know that we were directly overhead, and it was also a morale booster for the troops on the ground'. Capt McMahon also recalled that 'we'd come in almost supersonic, and it would scare them back into their holes'.

On one occasion, a B-1B was used to celebrate a more jubilant occasion following the fall of the Taleban, as Capt Morrison told the author. 'We were over Afghanistan, and the CAOC called us up and said "hey, there's this small village, very isolated, and the new regional governor is going to arrive" and they asked us for a flyby. So we did a high-speed, low-level pass as the regional governor rode in, accompanied by a contingent of Afghan National Army troops'. These low-level flypasts could be a challenge in themselves for the crews. Capt Morrison remembered that 'in certain parts of Afghanistan, the terrain is extremely mountainous. There are areas where the terrain-following radar doesn't work so well, and you have to keep that in mind. That was definitely a challenge'.

Capt Fessler recalled how convoy escort missions were run. 'We'd talk to the CAOC, and they'd be passing orders to us via satellite. We could also be tasked to talk directly to the guys on the ground. They would call us in and say "hey, we got this convoy which is going to be travelling from point 'A' to point 'B'" and they'd assign us a frequency and they would say contact this particular group on this frequency. We'd contact them and we'd escort them. If they ran into any trouble we'd obviously be on-call air support'.

Capt McMahon noted that 'we have a mode on our radar which can identify moving targets. We could identify Coalition convoys, but we didn't have the ability to positively identify targets'. It was not just route reconnaissance that the aircraft would perform. Capt Fessler remembers that 'we were sometimes used for weather reconnaissance to provide real-time information on what the weather was like in a particular part of the country'.

After loitering in the combat area, the crew would head for home. Once back at either Thumrait or Diego Garcia, the bomber was met by the crew chief and a team of around ten aircraft maintainers. The aircrew would then brief the maintenance team about the performance of the aircraft during the mission, while also informing them of any problems which they may have encountered.

The crew then headed to the Operations Building for debriefing, which usually took around an hour, and was performed in the presence of an intelligence officer. Senior Airman Michelle Utrecht, who was an intelligence operative with the 40th Expeditionary Operations Support Squadron, explained that 'upon returning from a combat sortie, the B-1 crew immediately met with us to discuss step-by-step what had occurred during their assigned mission from the time the jet left the tarmac to the moment the wheels touched down once again. Specifically, the aircrew informed us about the tactical events that made up their flight, which included surface-to-air fires and bomb-dropping'.

All of this added up to long days for the bomber crews. Capt Fessler recalled that 'there were occasions when the time between my arrival for work and the time I finished were over 24 hours. The biggest threat to us on such long days was staying alert. That was the toughest thing for me. However, staying alert was definitely not impossible, and all the crews did a very good job of coping with that stress'.

Work-share and automation played their part in helping the crews to stay sharp, as Capt Fessler explained;

'You could transfer control between the pilot and the co-pilot every half-an-hour or so, and the other guy at that point would act as an observer, looking outside the aeroplane to check that we were not getting shot at. There's a lot of things on board the jet which make it easier for us as well. We've got a computer into which we can programme orbits and holding patterns, and the aircraft will actually fly these orbits, which is good, because it gives your arms a rest. There is a downside to this too though, as if leave the aeroplane do everything, it does have a tendency to drift a little bit.

'On the way up there and back you could have one guy sleeping while the other one flew the jet, which was terrific, especially if you

The unmistakable shape of a Lancer high above the clouds. Initially in OEF the aircraft operated both in two-ship and single-ship configurations, organising strike packages in the air as and when they were needed. However, as the campaign developed, B-1Bs tended to operate alone for the majority of the time, as they would also do during OIF (*Capt Patrick McMahon*)

had showed up at two o'clock in the morning. A little nap on the way up was warmly received.

'As far as the mission tempo was concerned, on average I'd say each crew would probably fly once or twice a week. There were a couple of times when you'd do a flight, be down for a couple of days, and then be back up, but for the most part each crew would fly at least one mission a week. In addition to the flying, you also had other duties that you had to do on the ground in the mission planning cell'.

One of the longest missions flown in support of OEF was performed by a crew from the 37th EBS in December 2003. Capt Matt Brown, who was the Lancer commander on the mission, explained that 'this sortie was different from most other B-1B combat operations because of its duration. The sortie lasted a little less than 22 hours, involved six separate air refuellings and several classified operations'. On this mission, discovery of a Time-Sensitive Target (TST) meant that the bomber stayed longer over the battlefield than planned. 'The mission was evolving as we were in the air. The mission planners needed the B-1B with its weapons to execute the mission, and there were no other Lancers scheduled to replace us for six hours. Since the target was time-sensitive, they extended us'.

Such long missions can take their toll on the reaction time of the crew, which has to be razor-sharp. For this reason, the crew maximise their rest time during quiet periods. Lt Col Gary Mausolf, CO of the 37th EBS, commented that 'it's challenging to stay alert during long periods of inactivity, but when flying in-country, every crewmember is prepared and ready to execute the mission, no matter how tired they may be'.

34th BS 'Whizzo' Capt Kimberly Purdon remembered the long missions flown both in OEF and also in OIF;

'Our OEF commitment was maintained despite the commencement of OIF on 20 March 2003. That was the most tasked that we've been since OEF started in October 2001. The OEF missions can see us flying virtually anywhere in Afghanistan, and we can be instructed to loiter in-country anywhere between seven and sixteen hours, depending on the enemy's location. This period on-station comes on top of your pre-flight time, your mission briefing time, your debriefing time and all that stuff. Once you have taken all of this into account, you can easily log 20 hours for the day.

'You're wound up pretty good by the time you get back to base, and after taking a quick shower, you try and get your head down in your tent as quickly as possible. The next day, you're probably scheduled for something, but almost certainly not flying. You will typically get a day out of the cockpit because you've got to have twelve hours crew rest, but you will normally have other duties that you will have to do because there are so many things to be taken care of in respect to mission planning, and then you'd be right back into flying again. So there really wasn't much down time.'

In May 2004, a Lancer from the 40th AEG performed the longest mission for a B-1B in support of OEF. The gruelling 23-hour sortie was not intended to last that long, but the weather intervened, causing the aircraft to fly for longer than anticipated. Once airborne, the bomber was assigned to escort a military convoy south of Kabul. The aircraft escorted the convoy and successfully completed the mission, but as it headed home to Thumrait, a major dust storm moved into the area and the crew were obliged to divert to a different destination, probably Diego Garcia. The bomber's commander, Maj Mark Bennett, who was on his 17th combat mission, recalled that conditions were 'a little windy and a little rainy before we left, but there was no hint that things would be so bad when we returned'.

Three hours out of Thumrait, Maj Bennett called the base to check on the weather conditions, and he was told that a storm was well on its way. 'Conditions were rapidly degrading. At that point, we knew we had to get back as quickly as we could before the severe weather hit'. Behind Maj Bennett in the crew compartment was Capt Farley, the OSO. Flying his third combat mission, Farley had used the radar to detect any threats to the convoy on the ground. His skills were then turned to finding a safe path for the aircraft through the weather. 'The radar looked really bad for weather. We were zigzagging left and right to pick the best path through the storm'.

Once in the vicinity of the airfield, the crew had to decide whether to land, or to divert elsewhere. Staying in constant contact, Maj Bennett and the crew were given regular updates on the weather conditions at Thumrait. Meanwhile, on the ground another decision was being made about whether to send a tanker to rendezvous with the Lancer if the conditions further deteriorated so as to allow the aircraft to reach an alternate location.

This was a major undertaking, given that the tanker would probably be unable to land at its home base either once the storm moved in. 40th AEG Col Jeff Beene remembered that 'we launched the tanker with the intention that it would almost certainly be diverted as well. With the severe crosswinds at Thumrait, the tanker gave us much better options for getting the B-1B to a suitable location'.

B-1B crewman Capt Johnson, who was on his eighth combat mission, remembered that 'when they told us "we've got a tanker for you", that definitely made a difference. According to Maj Bennett, 75 miles from the base the weather was 'pretty dicey', but the crew were focused. 'You don't have time to worry. You're just concentrating on flying the best approach possible, while at the same time working out your other options if needed'. With less than ten miles to go before touchdown, the aircraft received the order to divert, although at that point the jet had still not met with the tanker. Capt Farley recalled that 'until we had the gas and were on the way, I was still a little concerned. There were a lot of things that still had to go right'.

With the bomber fuelled up, it was time to fly to the unnamed destination. Diplomatic sensitivities came into play, given that the B-1B was still loaded with weapons and had to fly through the airspace of several countries. Yet the condition of the bomber gave the crew some advantages. Crewmember Capt Clapp noted that 'it was a little unnerving' for the air traffic controllers en route, as they had to be informed that the aircraft was armed and lacking fuel, and in an emergency situation. These three things combined to allow the B-1B crew to navigate through third-party airspace without too many problems.

The 'Bones' were heavily reliant on the Air Force's overworked tanker force to allow them to remain on-station for hours on end over Afghanistan, not to mention the long transits to and from their home bases. Always in short supply and always in demand, the bombers and the tankers helped to keep the pressure on the Taleban (*B-1B Systems Program Office*)

Once on the ground, the aircrew had to get their jet refuelled and serviced in preparation for departure, which meant performing the duties usually done by maintainers. The bomber crews are trained to do this, but these procedures can still end up taking up to three hours to complete. Col Beene remembered that 'the sense of duty shown by this crew for getting the aircraft turned around and ready to go after a marathon mission like this is just incredible'.

With the storm having passed, and the flight home being uneventful, the crew finally got to their bunks. From the start of the mission, they had been awake for 38 hours. Capt Johnson told the author that 'I've never been up that long before. That was the longest day of my life'.

Long missions for the B-1B crews were a fairly regular occurrence, and one sortie for a bomber crew from the 9th EBS lasted more than 21 hours. The aircraft, which was commanded by Maj John Nichols, was called to patrol an area near Kandahar. Maj Nichols remembered that 'prior to the call for assistance, the situation was basically calm'.

After 14 hours of being airborne during an uneventful mission, the crew were cleared to return to Diego Garcia. Moments before the aircraft was to leave Afghan airspace, they received a call that ground units were embroiled in a firefight with AQT elements at a Coalition military compound. With other CAS aircraft refuelling at the time, and therefore unable to support the fight, a call came through asking the Lancer to assist.

The jet's DSO, Capt Christian Senn, recalled that 'this initiated a discussion amongst the crew members, and without batting an eye, we all agreed that we had to get involved. It had been a long day, but we had the fuel and weapons to help, and troops on the ground were in

A bright day in the desert and another mission gets underway. 85-0083 from the 34th BS prepares for another sortie, with the engines powering-up while another aircraft taxis to the runway (*B-1B Systems Program Office*)

harm's way. Did we get anxious? Absolutely. Three of the four on board were looking at our first combat strike – a big deal as an aviator'. Maj Nichols was the only member of the crew with previous combat experience.

Once they got to the combat area, the B-1B crew soon realised that they were in a difficult situation, given that AQT elements were adopting the time-honoured technique of 'hugging their enemy' – moving in so close to US troops that dropping ordnance in such conditions becomes extremely hazardous, with a high chance of a 'blue-on-blue' fratricidal event occurring. Capt Senn commented that 'dropping weapons over the heads of fellow Americans is just too dangerous, save in an emergency situation'.

The Lancer crew immediately notified the TAC of the proximity of the enemy cadres, and the danger of dropping the bomber's weapons in such conditions. The friendlies then moved south of the enemy's position so that the bomber could do its work. 'Another part of our training kicked in as a safety catch. We confirmed the target coordinates nearly half-a-dozen times to ensure that we were putting "iron" on the target, and not on our guys on the ground. We weren't going to have any mistakes'. What then followed was an uneasy quiet between the bomber releasing its weapons and the confirmation from

Lancer 86-0095 from the 77th BS prepares to take-off from runway 13/31 at Diego Garcia. During the early stages of the Afghan campaign there was nearly always one B-1B airborne in-theatre (*B-1B Systems Program Office*)

the ground that the attack had succeeded. 'There was a painfully long pause between the "thump" of the bombs leaving the aircraft and the TAC giving us his response. His voice finally broke the silence, and it was said as if with a smile – "direct hit"'.

A second strike, just to make sure that no one was left from the first attack, was planned, but the bomber's fuel situation meant that it was scrubbed. 'We began the second run, but could never get the final clearance to release. And therefore we could not make another drop. The other aircraft were back from refuelling and we were at "Bingo fuel", which was the minimum necessary to get back safely, so we were cleared to exit the area'.

Satisfaction and fatigue filled the cockpit as the crew headed home. Capt Senn remembered that 'as we left we were satisfied and extremely tired. We had been flying over Afghanistan for nearly ten hours'. The crew finally returned to base 21 hours after they had left. Once back on the ground, they learned just how effective the strike had been. Not only had six AQT fighters been killed in the strike, but up to $6 million of heroin had been vapourised.

These long sorties were both physically and mentally challenging to the Lancer crews. Capt Mark Chaisson flew missions during OEF and OIF, and he recalled how the crews managed to juggle their routines with the demands of the mission. 'When you're in country over hostile territory there is always a chance that someone's going to shoot you down, so you will always be strapped into your ejection seat during this stage of the mission. When we're flying those orbits or waiting for tasking, everybody is strapped in and ready to go in case something does impact the aircraft and you have to get out. You'd only be get up on your feet either straight after take-off or once we had left the combat area'.

Capt Purdon added that 'most people before they go in-country one-by-one would get out of their seats and do a quick stretch or use the restroom or something like that as they need to, knowing that once you got in-country you were strapped in with your helmet on in your ejection seat just in case anything happened. There are usually no more than one or two people out of their seat at any one time. When you're out of country, if you need to take a break you just tell the rest of the crew "hey I need a break. I need to clear off here and stretch my legs", so that the others can pay attention to what's going on'.

Capt Chaisson recalled that 'we were in-country for upwards of several hours, and you were in your seat for that entire time. You had your food and your water bottle right beside you, but there was no stretching your legs. Thos long missions took a real toll on the body'.

However, the most dramatic mission for any Lancer crew during OEF occurred on the night of 12 December 2001. B-1B 86-0114 *LIVE FREE OR DIE* was, according to its pilot Capt William Steele, 'flying a normally scheduled mission in support of the war. We then had multiple malfunctions, the jet went out of control and we all had to eject'. Capt Steele and his crew remembered the ejection vividly;

'Going through an ejection like that is about the most violent thing I've ever felt. We're all pretty bruised up and have some cuts. The way the B-1B ejection system works, you don't exactly go out all at the same time. It's sequenced to avoid interactions between hatches and seats and everything. However, it reacts very quickly, and you get all four crew members out in just a matter of seconds. The ejection sequence worked very well.

'Each crewmember sits on a Weber ACES II ejection seat which is the best in the world. But several five-second events have to go on to get us out of the aircraft – hatches have to go off the aircraft, and eventually our seats fire and we exit the aircraft. Basically, once you pull the ejection handles everything is automatic. I'm ejected out of the aircraft, my parachute opens automatically and my seat kit deploys with my life raft. So everything worked as it should have for me.'

The crew exited the aircraft at around 15,000 ft above the Indian Ocean. Capt Steele recalls that fear was very much in the back of his mind;

'We declared the emergency about 15 minutes prior to us having to eject. I actually wasn't scared at the time. I was just trying to go through all the emergency procedures that I could and then do my ejection sequence properly. I wasn't actually scared until I was in the parachute on my way down, because at the time of the accident I was trying my best to save the aircraft and the aircrew, and to do my job.'

Fortunately, a KC-10A from the 79th Air Refueling Squadron was taking off from Diego Garcia on an unrelated mission at that time, and its crew got the call that an inbound aircraft was in trouble. Maj Brandon Nugent, who was commanding the tanker, explained;

'As we were proceeding out, we heard the aircraft in distress returning to land, and we knew that they had a problem. The last thing we heard was that they were going to circle over the field and burn down some fuel. We didn't hear from them for a few minutes after that, and then we started picking up an emergency locator transmitter. We reported that, and after it was determined that they were out of radio contract, we then proceeded to the last known coordinates of the aircraft and started to search for them.

'Capt Dali was my co-pilot, and he had extensive training in search and rescue. Finally, the tanker's enlisted crewmen, Sgts Bero and Huhn, were instrumental in locating the rescue flares, beacons and strobe lights that were in the water. Once we did start locating them, Capt Dali was outstanding on the radios, coordinating with them and

The long transit times from Diego Garcia to Afghanistan, and the long time spent in orbits waiting for tasking, meant that tankers such as this KC-10A were indispensable. And it was a KC-10 which helped locate the crew of a crashed Lancer in December 2001 (*USAF*)

When on the ground, B-1Bs require unending and dedicated support from the maintainers to ensure that the bombers are always mission-capable – a far-cry from the mission capable rates which the aircraft experienced in the 1990s (*B-1B Systems Program Office*)

calling in all the other rescue aircraft and ships that came and actually picked up the downed crew.'

According to Maj Nugent, the atmosphere on the KC-10 was electric. 'There was extreme tension. We had about 20-25 minutes from the time that we started turning back towards the last known position until we actually got over the position. The pilot in the water apparently saw our lights and shot a flare. And when we saw that, we were extremely excited about it. And then shortly thereafter, Capt Dali was able to establish radio contact with the co-pilot of the downed jet'.

Capt Dali takes up the story of what happened once one of the crewmembers had been located;

'We determined which crew member it was – it happened to be the co-pilot from the B-1B. And the first thing that I wanted to know, being a former rescue guy, was what his physical condition was and what kind of signalling devices he had? So we had a conversation regarding his health, and it happened to be good, with just a small laceration to the face. Unfortunately, he had lost some of his equipment in the ejection, but he had one flare left. We established an orbit over the top of him at that point and stayed in constant communications. And once the boats got close enough, we had him pop that flare and the boat zoomed right in on him".

One of the B-1B crew commented that 'we were in the water for approximately two hours. And as far as communicating with the KC-10 and the rescue ship, we all carry our survival vests and a seat kit, which contains radios and several marking devices so that everybody can see us'. For Capt Steele, the ocean was not too inhospitable. 'Once in the water, we didn't see any hazards – no sharks or anything like that. Actually, it was kind of comfortable, it was nice warm water'.

The crew were dispersed over a wide area of ocean after the ejection. 'We were separated far enough that I could only see one other crew member. I was able to link up with my OSO, and we were just working together, trying to stay on top of our radio procedures and mark our positions for everybody coming to recover us. We also had a US Navy P-3 Orion out there assisting with our recovery. It was flying at a low altitude, searching for us with a spotlight. I was thankful to see everybody did get picked up'. The crew were plucked from the water by sailors manning a Rigid Hull Inflatable Boat despatched from the *Arleigh Burke* class destroyer USS *Russell* (DDG-59).

As far as the cause of the crash was concerned, a USAF inquiry failed to establish a reason for the accident, although it is possible that cockpit avionics may have displayed inaccurate attitude information, making it extremely difficult for the crew to control the aircraft.

Capt James Conley remembered a similarly nerve-racking mission after providing CAS to US ground troops;

'We had exited the combat area and were going to get fuel when we lost the number three engine. Down the line, we learned there was a malfunction on the jet and basically a part just failed. Of course we found this out *after* it had happened. What made it really interesting was because we had to leave Afghanistan so early, we were out of our cycles for our tankers, so we barely had enough fuel to make the different tanker tracks home, and we were continually on the radios requesting further tanker support.

'What ended up happening was that we ended up passing our inbound replacement "Bone" over the Indian Ocean, and we took about half the gas from his tanker that he was supposed to be using so

A KC-135R from the 319th ARW fills up a Lancer on its way to Afghanistan. Due to the long flight times from the B-1B's forward deployed operating bases to the Afghan theatre, the aircraft might have to be refuelled as many as four times during the sortie. Any excessive use of fuel by one aircraft, such as a particularly long sortie on account of bad weather, a requirement to strike a TST or mechanical difficulties such as an engine failure could cause repercussions in the Air Tasking Order if a tanker which was tasked with providing another aircraft with fuel was diverted to refuel a Lancer in difficulty. This made the balancing of the bomber assets with the tanker aircraft – both high-use platforms – a delicate affair (*USAF*)

B-1B Lancers bask in the desert heat at Thumrait. Having won their battle spurs over Afghanistan, these aircraft would win their wings over Iraq. 86-0113 from the 37th BS sits in the foreground, in front of an aircraft from the 9th BS/7th BW and other airframes from the 77th BS. To say that the 'Bone' scored an impressive tally in Afghanistan would be an understatement. Official USAF bombing statistics from the campaign state that Lancers dropped almost 40 per cent of the total ordnance tonnage expended during the first six months of OEF. This total included almost 4000 JDAM (67 per cent of the overall total used by Coalition forces). The aircraft also managed a 79 per cent mission-capable rate during this period (*USAF*)

we could get home. The outgoing B-1B did not go short of fuel, however, as the tanker that was supposed to be coming to refuel us on our way home as per our original mission plan ended up giving our replacement the remainder of his fuel. We spent a little while going "Okay, we're going to divert". It made for a very interesting sortie.'

Not a single 'Bone' was lost to enemy fire during OEF. Granted, the Taleban hardly possessed a highly sophisticated IAD system, but Man-Portable Air Defence Systems (MANPADS), which had been supplied by the Central Intelligence Agency to the Mujahideen during the Soviet intervention in Afghanistan two decades earlier, were a concern to the bomber crews nevertheless.

'The main threat to us was from shoulder-launched, infrared MANPADS, and you were always watching out for it. At low-level you could pre-empt any attack by using the countermeasures', explained Capt Morrison. The concern over air defences also depended where the aircraft was flying. Capt McMahon remembers that 'we were generally flying too high or too low or too fast for SAMs. The main concern was in the northeast of the country, where there were thought to be MANPADS'.

For the B-1B, OEF was the aircraft's 'coming of age', just as *Desert Fox* and *Noble Anvil* had seen the jet cutting its teeth as a robust and capacious bomber which was unexpectedly, yet ideally suited to the complex conflicts which have characterised the post-Cold War era. OEF would see the Lancer becoming the signature weapon of the conflict.

Lt Col Béen argues that 'the major lessons for OEF would be that we can very effectively do close air support and TST. We now also realise that there is a more permissive environment at high altitude. We reinforced those lessons in Iraq. With our loiter capability, massive internal load, speed and some pretty decent self-protection, we can be effective over the entire theatre. That's kind of what we've been preaching for years'.

These unique qualities were instrumental in turning the Taleban student militia and their al-Qaeda cohorts from being Afghanistan's power brokers to being on the run. The stage was set for the Lancer to play another crucial role in the second front of the 'Global War On Terror' (GWOT) – Operation *Iraqi Freedom*.

IRAQI FREEDOM

According to Air Marshal Sir Glenn Torpy, the RAF's UK Chief of Operations, 'for me, the B-1B was the star of OIF. It was an aircraft whose capabilities also got the RAF thinking that they might like something similar. I'm not saying we will now buy a fleet of long-range bombers, but for future procurements, we need to look at this type of capability'.

His praises were echoed by Lt Gen T Michael 'Buzz' Mosley, the Combined Forces Air Component Commander (CFACC) who shared Air Marshal Torpy's sentiments. 'Quite simply, the "Bone" was the most effective weapons system used during Operation *Iraqi Freedom*'. Using an American football analogy, Lt Gen Moseley described the aircraft as his 'roving linebacker' and 'weapon of choice' thanks to its flexibility, bomb-load, range, loiter time and aircrew willingness to 'stick their noses in the fight'.

Those Lancers participating in the removal of Saddam Hussein and his government were primarily based at Thumrait AFB, in Oman, and were operated by the 405th AEW. Wing vice-commander during OIF was Col Peter Kippie, who described what the Lancer brought to the fight. 'The B-1B was so flexible because of its long range and ability to carry more munitions than any other aircraft. We had a very dynamic capability to strike across the area of operations. There was no target within Iraq that was not at risk when we took off'.

The 405th AEW was technically a composite wing in that it operated more than one type of aircraft, including between ten and twelve Lancers at any one time, ten KC-135R tankers and between two and four E-3C AWACS aircraft.

The capabilities of the B-1B during the conflict were enhanced in no small measure on the ground by the hard work of the maintainers, who were able to keep the aircraft flying and were able to fix major problems on the bombers at a moment's notice. Their efforts to keep the Lancers airworthy acted as a *de facto* force multiplier, ensuring that there was always the maximum number of bombers in the air. Col Kippie added, 'We had broken aeroplanes on the first night, but they were repaired in an incredibly short time. We got every jet airborne and striking the targets when they should have been. Not a single B-1B was turned away either because of maintenance, threats or enemy defences'.

The 'Bones' would never have gotten airborne, let alone to their targets in OIF had it not been for the efforts of the maintainers on the ground. Looking after an aircraft as complex as the Lancer is a 24-hour job, and the abilities of the groundcrews to keep the aircraft airworthy acted as a force multiplier. 28th BS instructor pilot Maj Derek Leivestad was under no illusion as to how vital the ground staff were in getting the Lancers into the air during the campaign;

'The B-1B has proven in OEF and OIF the value of our capabilities, what we can do and what we can bring to the fight. But none of this would have happened had the maintenance folks not been on the flightline turning wrenches and loading the bombs. These guys performed phenomenally' (*B-1 Systems Program Office*)

The success of the Lancer in OIF won it plaudits both within and outside of the USAF. RAF officers were impressed with its capabilities, which have put high-speed, long-range bombers back on the air power agenda (*B-1B Systems Program Office*)

Capt Conley noted that 'one of the things about this aircraft is that when it stays at home, we have a low mission depletion rate. But if you look at this aeroplane in combat, the mission depletion rate becomes second-to-none. The real difference is the availability of parts. When we go overseas into combat, they give us the parts we need and the parts we should have, so things happen like they're supposed to.

'Historically, this airframe has been plagued by a lack of parts. Granted, over the years it's got a lot better because now we have a lot of these parts, and we're getting the funding that we never had. It's a maintenance-intensive aircraft, it's a sophisticated aircraft, and any sophisticated aircraft requires a lot of maintenance. Obviously, with our maintenance guys, they understand what's going on and they are very, very good at what they do.'

The weapon of choice during the campaign was the GBU-31 JDAM, which had proved itself in OEF. Col James M Kowalski, who commanded the 405th AEW during OIF, remembered the power of the Lancer/JDAM blow, along with the skills of the groundcrews;

'I knew we had a solid weapon with the JDAM combination of precision and punch, and with our defensive systems ranked among the best in the Air Force, allied to the jet's speed and manoeuvrability, we were very confident going into the war. Most importantly, we had a secret weapon – the world's best munition and maintenance folks.'

During the first 24 hours of the conflict (20-21 March), which was dubbed 'Shock and Awe', a series of pinpoint attacks were conducted against strategic targets in Baghdad and across Iraq. B-1Bs performed a number of these, with all ten Lancers assigned to the 405th AEW striking 240 planned targets with GBU-31 JDAM.

During the entire conflict, from 'Shock and Awe' until 1 May 2003, when President George W Bush officially declared the major combat phase of OIF to be over, the B-1B conducted 213 sorties (one per cent of the total number of sorties flown by Coalition aircraft), averaging eight missions of around eleven hours per day. The ordnance expended by the Lancers included 2159 JDAM – 43 per cent of the JDAMs dropped during the entire campaign, and 22 per cent of all of the guided weapons used throughout the conflict. All of the Lancer combat missions over Iraq, and elsewhere, were flown at an altitude of circa 20,000 ft – well out of the range of enemy SAMs and AAA.

B-1B OIF missions were also occasionally flown from Anderson AFB, on the Pacific island of Guam. B-1B 86-0121 *Symphony of DESTRUCTION* from the 37th BS had the double distinction of being the first 'Bone' over Baghdad and the performer of the longest Lancer mission in OIF (*Capt Michael Fessler*)

The 'Shock and Awe' phase of the war had been preceded by an attack a few days earlier on 14 March which had included Lancers. Flying as part of the OSW Air Tasking Order (ATO), two B-1Bs assigned to the 405th AEW, and presumably flying from Thumrait AFB, hit the H3 airfield complex, which was located some 250 miles west of Baghdad, as part of operations to enforce the southern No-Fly Zone. The bombers also hit nearby H2 airfield.

The targets bombed at each location included a mobile early warning radar and an air defence command centre which the Iraqi armed forces had recently moved into the zone. It was thought that these attacks greatly assisted Coalition forces – notably two British Special Air Service squadrons, a detachment from 45 Royal Marine Commandos and units from the US Army's 82nd Airborne Division and Delta Force – in their efforts to seize these bases once OIF began.

Interestingly, the Lancers had already been active in the Iraqi theatre during the hiatus between ODF and the commencement of OIF. Although the patrolling of the northern and southern No-Fly Zones over Iraq is synonymous with fighter and fighter-bomber aircraft, the

85-0087 of the 37th BS/28th BW departs a ubiquitous 'Forward Deployed Location' during OIF. Host nation sensitivity meant that the USAF kept extremely quiet about where exactly the 'Bones' were flying from during the campaign. However, the 'Forward Deployed Location' was taken in the B-1B's case to refer to Thumrait AFB, in Oman (*B-1B Systems Program Office*)

A sextet of Lancers return home to Ellsworth at the completion of OIF I. During the campaign, 28th BW jets operated from Thumrait, Diego Garcia and Guam. OIF and OEF taught the USAF several lessons about using the B-1B in the CAS role. While the aircraft was more than capable of performing this role, the B-1B community identified the Sniper XR targeting pod as a 'must have' addition for the future, as it would give the bomber the means to positively identify hostile targets. 'It really became apparent in Afghanistan and Iraq that we needed this capability' commented Lt Col George Raihala, deputy chief of projects at the B-1B Systems Group at Wright-Patterson AFB, in Ohio. The pod could be slaved to the B-1B's radar line-of-sight. When the bomber's radar identifies a possible target, the pod could be used to provide a clear visual image of the target. Installation of the pod would also mean that the bomber no longer has to call in a fighter with a similar capability to perform this task. However, the installation of a simple targeting pod might require the START treaty to be modified, given that this prohibits the use of the bombers' pylons, to which the Sniper would be mounted (*B-1B Systems Program Office*)

B-1B also participated in some of the patrols. Capt Mark Chaisson, who flew missions during OIF, says that the emphasis was not so much on the B-1B providing an on-call bombardment capability if required against Iraqi air defences, but was instead 'a familiarisation of the area. It was aimed at keeping the crews in the mindset of being ready for attack missions should they arise. Obviously, at the time, no-one had any idea if *Iraqi Freedom* was going to kick off or not, or when it was going to start. However, we knew that if it was going to, we would definitely be involved in it'.

Part of the Lancers' success during OIF was the change in the way the mission planning was performed for the aircraft. Traditional methods of generating 'scripted' sorties in which the crews were aware of their targets before they embarked on the missions were scrubbed in favour of a more flexible approach. Instead, the bomber crews could be handed their targets on their way to the Iraqi theatre, during their loiter time or on the way back to base. This was sometimes in addition to the targets which they had been allocated to attack before the mission had begun.

Should a flexible tasking be received in flight, the B-1B crews had to hastily organise *ad hoc* packages of SEAD support aircraft en route to the target. Capt Kimberley Purdon recalled that all of these unscripted missions were flown 'more or less in support of guys on the ground'.

The ability of the bomber to perform so flexibly was demonstrated on 21 March (Day Two of the conflict) when Lancer call-sign 'Walla 64' from the 405th AEW was tasked with attacking Republican Guard units to the south of Baghdad. The aircraft would soon find itself penetrating the city's legendary SuperMEZ – the heaviest air defence screens in Iraq. Maj Stephen Burgh, then a captain, and the OSO on the aircraft, remembered the mission well;

'It was the night of 21/22 March, and the B-1Bs hadn't gone "downtown" yet. We had got a call to help the US Army's 3rd Infantry Division, which was in southern Iraq, and we were supposed to hook up with a US Navy strike package. About 15 minutes before take-off, we got re-tasked to hit six GPS jamming towers which were affecting some of the weapons which the Coalition was using.'

Col Joe Brown was sitting in the co-pilot's seat, and alongside him, commanding the aircraft, was Capt Lee Johnson. Behind them were Capt Burgh and the DSO, Capt George Stone. Both of the crewmen 'up front' were using NVGs to navigate their way to the target area.

As the aircraft headed north on the two-and-a-half hour flight to Baghdad, Capts Burgh and Stone set about deciding on the best way to allocate the bomber's 24 JDAM so as to ensure total destruction of the multiple targets. They also had to make sure that the weapons would be used in such a way that collateral damage on the ground would be kept to a bare minimum – no easy task when employing 48,000 lbs of high explosive!

Targeting information was entered into the offensive avionics system and coordinates were continually rechecked to ensure that they were correct. En route, Col Brown rendezvoused with a KC-10A to replenish the bomber's fuel stocks, after which, as Maj Burgh remembered, 'we went straight into the SuperMEZ. We were the only asset going "downtown" that night. We got re-tasked with two F-16CJs and two EA-6B Prowlers. We had some reports of SA-2s and SA-3s firing ballistically. The AAA was thick, and I could have walked on it across Baghdad without touching the ground. You don't get a lot of visual references as a "Whizzo". I'd never seen a SAM launched before, and it looked like a huge telegraph pole. We manoeuvred, broke track and dropped our weapons'.

Flying in from the southeast corner of Baghdad, 'Walla 64' began its attack. Meanwhile, the EA-6Bs began to jam enemy air defences, while the F-16CJs remained on-station with their AGM-88 HARMs. The cloud deck was at around 10,000 ft, while the bomber was flying at 27,000 ft. Once the B-1B had flown across the city and away to the north, it began to get illuminated by several SAM radars.

The first set of towers was hit by a salvo of six JDAM, and the attack went according to plan. This was despite the fact that the crew saw AAA bursting all around the bomber. Yet the manoeuvrability of the Lancer made it relatively easy for the crew to avoid the concentrations of flak. The bomber then turned west and flew towards the centre of Baghdad. After the remaining JDAM had been released, Capt Johnson observed a SAM launch which caused Col Brown to immediately break left while Capt Stone released chaff and began to electronically jam the missile.

Once the second bomb run began, further manoeuvring was out of the question given that the aircraft had to maintain a steady heading in order to allow the JDAM to be sequentially released. However, the efforts of the DSO caused the SAM to eventually stop homing in on the bomber. The second missile broke its lock just 500 ft behind the aircraft, although the bomber was not yet out of danger given that heavy AAA continued to zoom past the aircraft. Maj Burgh recalled 'going onto our third target, we moved north. Right after we released on the third target, we had a guided missile shot at us, but we got lucky. It's a testament to the robust design of the aeroplane that we survived and got back. Not one B-1B came back with battle damage'.

The sum total of these efforts was that the bomber defeated four SAMs and avoided extremely heavy flak. A total of 23 of the aircraft's

24 JDAM were released against all six GPS-jamming towers, and their accompanying equipment. BDA after the attacks indicated that four of the towers had been completely destroyed, along with one tower suffering light damage. No anti-GPS emissions were detected for the duration of OIF, which indicates that 'Walla 64's' efforts had been successful. Even if the Iraqis had wished to jam the GPS signals which the Coalition were using for bombing, Col James Kowalski went on record at the time stating that this amounted to a wasted effort;

'If the Iraqis are spending money to buy this stuff, they're wasting their cash. JDAM has an inertial navigation system, so even if it fails to get a lock on the GPS signal, it's going to land within about 40 ft of its target.'

The strength of Iraqi air defences at any given moment seemed almost impossible to predict for the crews. There were occasions when the AAA and SAMs lit up Baghdad like a proverbial Christmas tree, yet there were other times when the defences would be dormant. Capt Chris Wachter, who would fly on one of the most important Lancer missions during the conflict, recalled that 'I've flown on missions that went right over the heart of Baghdad, where there were known air defence threats, and seen absolutely nothing – no one was shooting at me. Other times, it was kind of non-stop'.

As far as the crews were concerned, they always assumed that the defences would be heavy. 'Whizzo' Capt Ty Newman noted that 'the threat was certainly out there, and on any given mission we took every precaution, and used all our tactics, to minimise the threat to our aircraft as we went on strikes inside Baghdad'.

Part of the key to negating the air defences was the provision of dedicated SEAD support assets which would join the strike package en route to Baghdad. EA-6B Prowlers were indispensable, saturating enemy air defences with electronic interference, while F-16CJs and F/A-18Cs would play their part firing AGM-88 HARM missiles in the vital 'Wild Weasel' role which had been the preserve of the USAF's F-4G Phantom IIs in *Desert Storm*. Just as vital were the E-3C AWACS aircraft, who provided battle management, and the 'big wing' KC-10A and/or KC-135R tankers.

When discussing the efficacy of the 'Bone's' defensive avionics during OIF, Capt Purdon commented that 'with the ALQ-161, you put in the chaff and you put in the flare decoy system altogether, and

Lancer 86-0117 of the 28th BS/7th BW lifts off from the runway at Diego Garcia. Throughout the major combat phase of OIF, the Lancers were tasked with hitting strategic targets and performing CAS missions similar to those undertaken in Afghanistan. One B-1B pilot discussed the process of using the bomber as a CAS platform in Iraq, particularly in urban operations, where friendly and enemy forces are often in close proximity. 'Training really does take over and time slows down. You double and triple check everything. As a crew, you make sure your coordination is tip-top. It's great to know that in about five seconds, when the clock runs out, the bad guys are going to die and the good guys will be okay' (*B-1B Systems Program Office*)

All geared-up for the Baghdad SuperMEZ, this B-1B is having its JDAM-packed Conventional Rotary Launcher carefully installed into its rear weapons bay. The 'death by a thousand cuts' which US and British aircraft had managed to inflict on the Iraqi Integrated Air Defence System had helped to severely degrade Saddam's abilities to protect himself from air attacks. This did not stop B-1B crews taking the threat extremely seriously, however, and Lancers were targeted on several occasions as they went 'downtown'. Following its participation in the conflict, the Lancer was dubbed the 'Most Valuable Aeroplane' according to Maj Leivestad. 'We're the big kids on the block because of what battlefield commanders are saying now – "If the plan doesn't involve the B-1Bs, I don't want it"' (*B-1B Systems Program Office*)

they did a very good job with the threat we had to deal with in OIF and OEF'.

Despite the efforts of maintainers, accidents did occur during the campaign. The worst one saw $1.3-million worth of damage caused to a 34th EBS bomber which was improperly loaded with JDAM prior to flying an OIF mission. It was reported that the Lancer's bombs were not loaded evenly, causing rivets on the rotary launcher to fail.

If the bombing of Hiroshima and Nagasaki put the B-29 Superfortress into the public eye, then a Lancer mission on 7 April 2003 arguably performed the same feat for the B-1B. Aircraft commander Capt Chris Wachter, co-pilot Capt Sloan Hills, OSO Lt Col Fred Swan and DSO Lt Joe Runci were orbiting in their Lancer 86-0138 *SEEK AND DESTROY* over central Iraq when the crew received notification that Saddam Hussein and his sons Qusay and Uday were meeting at a restaurant in the al-Mansour district of southwest Baghdad.

The bomber, which was part of the 28th BW, was immediately instructed to target the restaurant with a stick of 2000-lb GBU-31 JDAM. The attack saw a symbolic shortening of the famed 'sensor-to-shooter' time, with the bomber releasing its weapons just 12 minutes after receiving its orders. Such an attack, it was hoped, could shorten the campaign by obtaining the strategic effect of decapitating the Iraqi regime – a key objective of OIF.

The entire attack, from the time that the tip was received until the bombs were dropped took just 47 minutes. At the time, it was said that the attack could have been completed even sooner had officials further up the chain of command not become absorbed in debates over whether or not to execute the strike. During these 47 minutes, the intelligence tip-off was passed from the field firstly to the CAOC at Al Udeid, in Qatar, then to the National Imagery and Mapping Agency, where the precise coordinates of the restaurant were established, then back to the CAOC, and from there to an E-3 AWACS, which tasked *SEEK AND DESTROY* with the mission.

At the time they received the coordinates, the bomber was flying in a loiter pattern over western Iraq. The aircraft had just been refuelled by a tanker when it received the order to proceed to a critical target in

Baghdad. The only indication that the crew had as to the importance of the target was a tip from the Battle Manager on board the AWACS that this was 'the Big One'. Lt Col Swan takes up the story;

'We got the target set through Airborne Communications, and we confirmed these coordinates. It then took us about 12 minutes to fly to the target and release the weapons. The atmosphere on the flight deck was tense. When we got the word that it was a priority leadership target, we initially experienced an adrenalin rush, but then we reverted back to our original training, which says "hey, let's get the job done". We knew that we had to react quickly, and for me, I was thinking "this could be the big one, so let's make sure we get it right". Once the coordinates were entered into the aircraft's offensive avionics, it was time to turn towards the target area and prepare for the bomb run.'

The aircraft then expended its weapons – four to be precise. The first to be dropped were two GBU-31(V)3/B weapons. These munitions have a hard target penetration ability which meant that they would burrow into the ground before exploding. They were followed by two GBU-31(V)1/B weapons, which had a 25-millisecond delay before exploding. Essentially, the first two bombs would penetrate the target if it was heavily defended and would explode, making room for the next two weapons, which would explode in the unlikely event that anyone or anything was left after the first blasts.

The use of penetrating munitions during OIF gave targeting planners much more flexibility, given that they were able to cut down the size of a munition as less blast would be needed to defeat any protection which surrounded the target. 'A little more useful for the planners when they look into a dense environment' said Col Kowalski.

While the 12 minutes taken to strike Saddam's meeting place was fast, it could have been even faster, perhaps taking as little as six minutes from the receipt of the order until the bomb drop, had the B-1B decided to 'dash' at its supersonic velocity of circa Mach 1.2. As it was, the bomber flew at subsonic speeds to its target.

The work for Lt Col Swan and his colleagues on this flight was by no means complete following the restaurant strike, and two additional targets were hit. Lt Col Swan recalled that 'One of the targets was actually a surface-to-air missile site that was suspected or confirmed, and then we went and killed it. The other was an airfield that we went and struck as our third target for the day'. Some 17 JDAM were dropped in these two strikes, Lt Col Swan remembering that 'in general, we had two different target groups, and we had nine weapons on one and eight on the other. They were probably 200 miles apart'.

For the crew, it was all in a day's work. 'We did all that during the course of a sortie that lasted ten-and-half-hours' explained Lt Col Swan. He also mentioned that 'attacking a priority leadership target isn't like attacking an ammunition dump. It has a different feel to it. We understand the situation. It's not like you're some detached being up there just throwing weapons out. There's a lot of thought going into what you're doing, and for the safety of people on the ground'.

During the conflict, a Lancer was permanently loitering over western Iraq waiting for orders to strike at TSTs as and when they were located. As one bomber was loitering, another would be en route to the

Just as it had done in Afghanistan, the B-1B/GBU-31 combination delivered the one-two hit that was sufficient to leave both Iraqi battlefield and leadership targets punch-drunk, destroyed and demoralised. An aircraft from the 34th BS waits on the ramp in the background (*B-1B Systems Program Office*)

orbiting location, ready to relieve it, while a third aircraft, which had also been loitering, would be on its way back to Thumrait. All of this added up to one Lancer being permanently stationed over western Iraq ready to respond at speed with precision weapons. Col Kowalski described this 'to-ing and fro-ing' of bombers into and out of Iraqi airspace as 'synchronised ballet' with the bombers providing a 'suffocating presence' over the Iraqi theatre. Maj Burgh noted that the mission tempo 'was non-stop. There was a lot of adrenalin and for just under a month we were continually doing it'.

Eric Branum, programme manager with the B-1 Systems Group at Wright-Patterson AFB, argued that 'when you look at the Lancer's tremendous capability to drop conventional weapons, and you combine that with its speed and loitering ability, the addition of positive ID capability really becomes a critical factor in meeting the Chief of Staff's objectives of reducing the (find, fix, track, target, engage, assess) kill chain cycle'.

The evidence for the responsiveness of the Lancer could be seen in the amount of targets which were pre-planned and issued to bomber crews when they were still on the ground, and those which were handed off to them once they were in flight, or in the case of 'Walla 64', when they were heading out to the runway. Only 36 per cent of the bomber's targets were pre-planned and were included in the ATO – the daily 'sheet music' from which the OIF air war would be conducted. The other two-thirds were allotted to crews once in flight. It was not unheard of for a B-1B returning to base after loitering over western Iraq to be tasked with hitting a target on its way home too.

One of the major missions for the loitering Lancers was to provide a rapid response to the discovery of Scud, Al Samoud 2, FROG-7 or Ababil mobile missile launchers (either stored or active). Coalition planners were desperate to avoid a re-run of *Desert Storm*, when Coalition aircraft and Special Forces were unable to destroy a single Scud missile during the conflict, and Saddam was able to lob missiles against Saudi Arabia and Israel at will.

The B-1B was not ideally suited to this role, however, as Col Kowalski explained. 'In Iraq, we used the B-1B's Ground Moving Target Indicators to look for Scuds out in the western desert, but its resolution was insufficient to positively ID them as targets. I would then have to call in a fighter with a targeting pod to look at it and tell me what it was we had found'.

In terms of TSTs, there were three categories of target – leadership targets (senior government or military officials), which absorbed 50 Lancer missions; WMD targets, which accounted for 102 TST missions; and strikes against terrorists, four of which were flown. The remaining 57 missions flown saw B-1B crews providing CAS for troops on the ground.

The aft area of the Lancer houses the defensive electronics and countermeasures that enabled the bomber to defeat the robust air SAM and AAA defences which surrounded Baghdad (*B-1B Systems Program Office*)

The typical OIF mission mix of hitting TSTs and ad hoc targets during the course of a single sortie was perhaps best illustrated by the experiences of a B-1B crew that was tasked with attacking a time-sensitive leadership target and then re-rolling to defeat Republican Guard forces that had friendly troops pinned down. Tasking for the latter was passed to the crew when they were already on their way back home, the bomber receiving a frantic radio call for help directly from the troops involved. The aircraft diverted to their position, coordinated with a TAC on the ground and attacked the Iraqi units.

Capt Chaisson vividly remembered his CAS missions during OIF;

'Basically, a FAC/TAC would call us in against the targets of opportunity. The troops would be in contact with the enemy, or there would be a situation where they knew that they had a target that needed to be taken out, and the GBU-31 was a good weapon to do

JDAM await loading into Conventional Rotary Launchers from their bomb trolleys at Anderson AFB during OIF (*USAF*)

just that. That's pretty much what we did.'

The GBU-31 was the weapon of choice for all the Lancer missions during OIF. According to Capt Purdon, 'JDAM is our money-maker because of its size, and because its GPS near-precision capability takes away the error factor'. Capt Chaisson recalled that his jets 'didn't carry anything but JDAM. That's what we had, and that's what they asked us to use. Obviously, it minimised the most collateral damage because it's near precision-guided, so we pretty much hit what we were shooting at, and that's what everybody wants'.

A B-1B cruises in the skies high above Iraq. As in Afghanistan, the ability of this aircraft to loiter and strike proved fatal to the enemy (*B-1B Systems Program Office*)

For the 'Whizzos', JDAM presented its own challenges, given that targets would be handed to the crews while they were airborne. Capt Purdon remembered that 'once you got the airborne tasking, the "Whizzo" and I had to manage and allocate targets to all of those 24 weapons, and arrange where the location of those targets was. It took both of the "Whizzos" in the back seats to do that, to "quality control" it and to make sure that we weren't making any errors. There were checks and balances in place the entire time to make sure that we weren't making any mistakes in the allocation of the targets'.

Col Kowalski described what OIF missions were like for the crews;

'Most of the time we would simply go up there, hit some targets and find a tanker. While we were on the tanker we would get additional targets, and then go strike again.'

This was made possible by the technological changes which had occurred at the command and control level, particularly in the abilities of the CAOC. The battlefield in Iraq could move rapidly, and the tasking of the bombers would have to keep up with that, as Col Kowalski confirmed;

'Sometimes the front moved so fast we were getting additional targets after we had entered Iraqi airspace. We were using satellites to transmit targeting data – basically e-mails from the CAOC that updated us with TSTs. We have all the players linked up now. It allows us to react much more quickly to changes on the battlefield and to what we detect via intelligence.'

Lancer 85-0085 of the 37th BS/28th BW deposits its crew back at Ellsworth AFB after a deployment overseas. A station wagon painted in the tiger stripes of the 37th BS can just be seen behind the crew bus (*Senior Airman Michael Keller*)

Ellsworth base firefighters welcome home B-1B crews on 13 May 2003. Six jets, and their crews, returned to a crowd of family and friends welcoming them home (*USAF*)

All of this would amount to dashes across the 'football field' of Iraq at a moment's notice;

'To run the distance of the field was quite a test. It was not unheard of to quickly send a crew more than 200 miles north to support Special Operations Forces engaged with the enemy, and then coordinate additional priority targets for the crew to attack out west on their way home.'

The ability of the B-1B to react so quickly to TSTs, along with its range and payload, which had been so ably demonstrated in the skies of Afghanistan, illustrated that the Lancer had now thoroughly matured as a conventional platform. The aircraft had the distinction of coming within a hair's breadth of killing the Iraqi leader, his two sons and other senior Iraqi officials – a key objective of OIF – and had the sensor-to-shooter time been quicker, it might have succeeded. On this occasion it did not, but it showed that this aircraft could act as a 'flying sniper rifle' as well as a 'bomb truck'.

True, the B-1B did have shortcomings in OIF. It had difficulty hitting mobile ballistic missile launchers, for example, but these were problems which can be solved should the aircraft receive further modifications to allow it to attack such targets.

Should there be either another conflict in the Global War on Terror, a more conventional war of the sort seen during *Desert Storm*, an asymmetric campaign against al-Qaeda-style elements in a failed state or a combination of the two, it is almost certain that if the USAF is involved, then the Lancer will be too. The bomber's combat record shows that it is an aircraft which has confounded its critics on four occasions, and has become as versatile a bomber as its B-52H cousin.

B-1B 86-0095 of the 77th BS/28th BW at Ellsworth AFB sits on the ramp behind its sister aircraft 86-0113 of the 37th BS/28th BW upon their arrival home from OIF/OEF on 13 May 2003. The CAS and TST missions which the B-1B has performed so well in the Global War on Terror have been introduced into exercises such as the 2005 *Cope Thunder* initiative in Alaska. This event featured large strike package employment missions in which the B-1B participated, flying in from CONUS and overseas bases (*B-1B Systems Program Office*)

THE FUTURE

B-1B 86-0104 from the 37th BS/28th BW departs the runway at Ellsworth. The Lancer is set to enjoy a productive future in the USAF inventory thanks to the vital role it has played in conflicts following the end of the Cold War. The ceaseless business of keeping the jet sharp continues, and in 2005 $5 million of funding was secured to improve the bomber's secure communications. This will see the installation of systems such as the ARC-210 radio (*28th BW*)

Where does the B-1B Lancer go from here? Having earned its impressive reputation in the Balkans, the Gulf and Afghanistan, the 'Bone' has thoroughly established itself as an indispensable aircraft for the USAF as it fights today's wars and prepares to fight tomorrow's.

Capt Kimberley Purdon recalled that one of the major consequences of the bomber's participation in all of these conflicts was that they 'completely wiped out the conventional theory of how you attach target coordinates to a crew before you take off. Prior to OEF, I needed to know where I was attacking because I had to plan for the mission. Now, operational doctrine basically says "hey, you can take-off, you're going to go here, you're going to sit and I'm going to give you targets via secure e-mail, secure communications or voice communications, and you're going to go and do it all in real time". So it takes the conventional carpet bombing, pre-planned, target theory and throws it out of the window. It also shows that the B-1B and the B-52H can easily flex in a heartbeat to something new, do it right and do it well'.

The aircraft may receive additional upgrades to prolong its life. The USAF has still to decide whether it will replace its present, and ageing, heavy bomber fleet with a new manned aircraft, or whether it will go for an entirely new capability such as an unmanned strike platform. Capt Mark Chaisson told the author that 'we're always looking for upgrades if we can get them – particularly upgrades to increase the usability and flexibility of the aircraft. Looking down the road, the more of those we can procure the better. As far as proving our capability, the type of conflicts that may arise in the future could be very similar to the ones that we have just fought. If that is indeed the case, then we need to continue what we're doing now'.

Casting an eye to the future of warfare, Capt Purdon argues that 'previous to these conflicts, there was no doubt that everyone was speculating that the B-1B was on its way out. In OEF and OIF, we were able to prove ourselves. There's a lot of different jobs that the B-1B can do. Everyone knows that the future will see much more urban warfare, where you can't pick out your friend from your enemy. Can we get the weapons to go and help out the troops in a "danger close" environment, and if so, can we actually perform this mission? Maybe that will be something we go and do in the future'.

As part of the CMUP, the B-1B is in line to receive several new weapons systems during its Block E series of upgrades. First to be integrated will be the AGM-158 Joint Air-to-Surface Stand-off Missile (JASSM). Its integration with the aircraft, as with all weapons systems retrofitted to the Lancer, is easier said than done, however.

The jet's designers never envisaged the aircraft having such a prominent conventional role, and the integration of the AGM-158 is not expected to be complete across the Lancer fleet until 2007. Once reworked, each bomber will be able to carry 24 of these weapons, launching them from as far away as 192 miles from their targets. The aircraft will be able to carry both the A and B variants of the missile, the latter having a longer range of up to 559 miles, and a correspondingly larger fuel load. Moving forward to the 2015 timeframe, it is entirely possible that the Lancer will be given a completely new radar.

Other improvements could include the addition of a Sniper XR targeting pod. The B-1B Systems Group is currently designing modifications for the bomber so that it can use such equipment. As mentioned in the previous chapter, the need for the targeting pod was identified during OIF when the aircraft was used to target mobile ballistic missile launchers but lacked the ability to positively identify them when located. Lt Col George Raihala, Deputy Chief of the

The capacious weapons bay of a Lancer, with a JDAM located aft of the partition. While the bomber has used the GBU-31 as its 'money-maker', it is scheduled for qualification on a new series of weapons. The Joint Air-to-Surface Stand-off Missile will be deployed on the aircraft. Crucially, the bomber will also have the capability to launch more than one weapons type in a single mission. This is a vital capability, as it will allow the aircraft to engage a wider variety of targets on a single mission, rendering the B-1B an even more potent weapons system. The Small Diameter Bomb (SBD) is also a possibility for inclusion in the 'Bones'' growing arsenal of weaponry. However, the USAF will have to decide which weapons system is the most pressing priority, and orders of one may have to be cut in order to provide adequate numbers of the other. For instance, the JASSM is most effective against a potential aggressor with a well-developed IADS, and at present only China really falls into this category. The SBD, however, is likely to be far more effective in the kind of counter-insurgency operations that US forces are presently involved with (*Senior Airman Michael Keller*)

Project Division at the B-1B Systems Group, believes that 'it really became apparent in Afghanistan and Iraq that we needed this capability'.

The idea is for the pod to be 'slaved' to the B-1B's radar line-of-sight. When an item of interest is picked up on the radar, the possible target's coordinates can then be fed into the pod in order to obtain a clear visual image of the target. The pods are expected to be fully integrated by around 2009, and according to Lt Col Raihala, 'with the way warfare is currently moving, putting Sniper XR on the B-1B will reap huge benefits in the future'. Maj Burgh agrees that this is a necessary addition;

'There's not a lot of understanding as to how good this aeroplane is. The pod would give us an even more robust capability. The only thing we do at the moment is radar bombing. If we could do it ourselves, we could identify something even if the ground troops couldn't.'

Capt James Conley believes that 'one of the assets we would have as a FAC-A qualified aircraft is four crewmembers on board, and part of the FAC-Air role is not only cueing to strike targets, but relaying target coordinates and stacking other aircraft appropriately. If there's four people in the aircraft, then that becomes a lot easier. There's a lot of things we can do with the B-1B, given the right upgrades'.

For Capt Chaisson, the major lesson learnt by the Lancer community, and the USAF at large, was that 'nobody expected the B-1B to be such an overarching CAS platform. Many of the services weren't prepared to deal with us in that role, especially coming into OEF. People that were on the ground were not prepared, and typically never considered a heavy bomber as a CAS aircraft, capable of pin-point strikes against enemy forces that were engaging our troops. So our exposure to the CAS mission alone has really changed what we do, and it's changed the way that we train too. But that's just one aspect of it.

'Troop commanders on the ground went from being "Okay, we're going to call them if we need to hit a heavy target, or if we need to drop lines of weapons" to "Okay, we can have them orbiting all the time, ready to engage the enemy at a moment's notice". We've got a lot of weapons and a lot of gas, and we can hang out for a long time.'

Capt Conley explained that 'we don't do CAS as a typical fighter does. We've got radar, and knowing how the Tactical Air Control Party (TAC-P) works, and how the aircraft works, makes it easy to be talked onto the target because you understand what the TAC-P's looking for. You understand what the airframe's doing, and you can make it actually happen. Ironically enough, when you do it right, you actually perform the FAC mission more expeditiously than a fighter'.

However, Capt Conley, who has worked as a TAC as well as a B-1B crewman, still believes that there are lessons which need to be learned in the Lancer community if the aircraft is going to become a more potent CAS platform;

'I lot of the time I would hear things on the radio and I could quickly understand what was happening. Indeed, I often taught the other guys in my crew the CAS "language". A good example is when the Army says "destroy or neutralise", which means that they just want

On the taxiway and ready to go, a 28th BW Lancer prepares for another sortie over Iraq. By the time the CMUP is fully completed, the aircraft will be able to carry one of the most versatile weapons loads in the USAF, which is sure to make it yet more attractive to CFACCs in future conflicts. At the time of writing, the Pentagon had recommended the closure of Ellsworth AFB and the moving of the entire B-1B fleet to Dyess. This was rejected by the Defense Base Closure and Realignment Commission, which has insisted that Ellsworth will stay open. The US Congress is also recommending that the USAF reactivate the Lancers which are currently languishing in storage. This is something which could be extremely expensive for the USAF to do, given the cost of bringing old bombers up to the standard of deployed aircraft vis-a-vis recent upgrades (*28th BW*)

the target moved out of sight. In Air Force parlance, it means that you turn the target into a piece of metal! They're small differences, but they're enough'.

One of the other 'issues' which the aircraft has at present is that the 'money-making' weapon which is carried by the B-1B, namely the GBU-31 JDAM, is too powerful for most urban CAS situations. Capt Conley explained;

'The weapon is too big, so we can't get in right and tight like you can do with a GBU-38 500-lb JDAM-equipped fighter. The GBU-31, because it's a 2000-lb weapon, does limit what we can and can't do. A smaller weapon would actually give us a lot more capability. One of the major things we're looking at right down the road is getting clearance to employ the GBU-38.'

In the 20th anniversary year of the B-1B entering service with the USAF, and just over seven years since the jet saw combat for the first time, the Lancer stands as an aircraft which has comprehensively reinvented itself to become an indispensable weapons system. Perhaps the final word on the B-1B's past, present and future should go to Capt Michael Fessler;

'The B-1 was originally designed as a low-level nuclear penetrator, so obviously in the 1990s, when that role went away, it was doubtful that the aircraft would make anything of itself. The last thing that people had really heard about the B-1B was how it was plagued with problems, and how big and expensive it was. It was kind of a dinosaur, so to speak.

'When we began flying the missions that we were doing in Afghanistan and Iraq, it really brought to light that the B-1B is an essential platform for our forces. We carry a lot of weapons. We can use it as a CAS platform and we can use it as a surgical bomber. We had an astonishing amount of firepower on-call anytime, anywhere. Our exploits in the Global War on Terror have, to date, convinced the US government and the Air Force that this is a platform they should want to keep around, and that we are capable of so much more.'

APPENDICES

APPENDIX A

B-1B FLEET LIST

The total production run for the B-1B Lancer totalled 99 aircraft, of which 65 are still in service with the 9th, 13th, 28th, 34th, 37th and 77th BSs at Dyess and Ellsworth AFBs, and the 419th Flight Test Squadron at Edwards AFB. The remaining airframes are distributed between AMARC and aircraft museums throughout the United States. The rest have been written-off in accidents.

CURRENT SQUADRON ASSIGNMENT AS OF NOVEMBER 2005

9th BS/7th BW, DYESS AFB

Aircraft production number	Lot	Serial number	Name
24	4	85-0064	*Wichita Intertribal Warrior Society*
32	4	85-0072	*Polarized*
48	4	85-0088	*Phoenix*
49	4	85-0089	*POW MIA Some Gave All and All Gave Some*
63	5	86-0103	*The Reluctant Dragon*
70	5	86-0110	*Better Duck*
72	5	86-0112	*Black Widow*
80	5	86-0120	*Iron Horse*
83	5	86-0123	*Let's Roll*
84	5	86-0124	*Georgia Guardian*
95	5	86-0135	*Deadly Intentions*
100	5	86-0140	*Last Lancer*

13th BS/7th BW, DYESS AFB

Aircraft production number	Lot	Serial number	Name
29	4	85-0069	*Home Improvements*
33	4	85-0073	*Dark Knight*
34	4	85-0074	*Crew Dawg*
50	4	85-0090	*Hellcat*
60	5	86-0100	*Phoenix*
65	5	86-0105	*The 8th Chadwick*
67	5	86-0107	*Dragon Slayer*
69	5	86-0109	*Spectre*
82	5	86-0122	*Antidote*
97	5	86-0137	*Ace in the Hole*

28th BS/7th BW, DYESS AFB

Aircraft production number	Lot	Serial number	Name
19	4	85-0059	*Justice for All*
21	4	85-0061	*Maverick*
25	4	85-0065	*Lil' Chief*
40	4	85-0080	*West Texas Fury*
58	5	86-0098	*Midnight Train from Georgia*
61	5	86-0101	*The Watchman*
68	5	86-0108	*Alien with an Attitude*
77	5	86-0117	*Night Stalker*
79	5	86-0119	*The Punisher*
86	5	86-0126	*Hungry Devil*
90	5	86-0130	*Bad Company*
92	5	86-0132	*Oh Hard Luck*
93	5	86-0133	*Old Crow Express III/Memphis Belle*
96	5	86-0136	*Special Delivery*

34th BS/28th BW, ELLSWORTH AFB

Aircraft production number	Lot	Serial number	Name
20	4	85-0060	*Dakota Posse*
43	4	85-0083	*Overnight Delivery*
44	4	85-0084	*Hard Rain*
78	5	86-0118	*Iron Mistress*
89	5	86-0129	*Black Widow*
94	5	86-0134	*Doolittle Raiders*
98	5	86-0138	*Seek and Destroy*
99	5	86-0139	*Vanna*

37th BS/28th BW, ELLSWORTH AFB

Aircraft production number	Lot	Serial number	Name
26	4	85-0066	*No Antidote II*
41	4	85-0081	*After Shock*
45	4	85-0085	*Intimidator*
47	4	85-0087	*Screamin' for Vengeance*
53	5	86-0093	*Global Power*
54	5	86-0094	*Night Hawk*
59	5	86-0099	*Haulin' Ass*
62	5	86-0102	*Bad Moon*
64	5	86-0104	*American Flyer*
71	5	86-0111	*Ace in the Hole*
73	5	86-0113	*Jagged Edge*
76	5	86-0116	*Victress*
81	5	86-0121	*Symphony of Destruction*
87	5	86-0127	*The Kansas Lancer*

77th BS/28th BW, ELLSWORTH AFB

Aircraft production number	Lot	Serial number	Name
37	4	85-0077	*Screamin' Eagle*
39	4	85-0079	*Master of Disaster*
51	4	85-0091	*Freedom's Vengeance*
55	5	86-0095	*Dakota Demolition*
57	5	86-0097	*Iron Eagle*
75	5	86-0115	*Top Secret*
85	5	86-0125	*Swift Justice*

419th FLIGHT TEST SQUADRON/412th TEST WING, EDWARDS AFB

Aircraft production number	Lot	Serial number	Name
9	3	84-0049	*Thunder from the Sky*
28	4	85-0068	
35	4	85-0075	

AEROSPACE MAINTENANCE AND REGENERATION CENTER, DAVIS-MONTHAN AFB

Aircraft production number	Lot	Serial number	Name and squadron/bomb wing
10	3	84-0050	*Dawg B-one* – 28th/7th
13	3	84-0053	*Lucky 13* – 13th/7th
14	3	84-0054	*Rage* – 28th/7th
15	3	84-0055	*Lethal Weapon* – 28th/7th
16	3	84-0056	*Sweet Sixteen* – 28th/7th
18	3	84-0058	*Eternal Guardian* – 9th/7th
22	4	85-0062	*Uncaged* – 9th/7th
27	4	85-0067	*On Defense* – 28th/7th
30	4	85-0070	*Excalibur* – 77th/28th
31	4	85-0071	*Mr Bones* – 128th BS, Georgia Air National Guard
42	4	85-0082	*Global Power* – 419th FLTS
46	4	85-0086	*Soaring with Eagles* – 37th/28th
52	4	85-0092	*Apocalypse* – 128th BS, Georgia Air National Guard
56	5	86-0096	*Wolfpack* – 28th/7th
57	5	86-0097	*Iron Eagle* (returned to service with 28th BW 9/04)
88	5	86-0128	*Fury 1* – 37th/28th
91	5	86-0131	*Guardian* – 77th/28th

B-1B LOSSES

Aircraft production number	Lot	Serial number	Unit, Name and loss data
12	3	84-0052	96th BW, (no name) crashed near La Junta, Colorado, 28 September 1987
17	3	84-0057	7th BW, *Hellion*, crashed at Dyess AFB, 12 February 1998
23	4	85-0063	96th BW, (no name) crashed at Dyess AFB on 4 October 1989
36	4	85-0076	28th BW, *Black Jack*, crashed at Ellsworth AFB on 18 November 1988
38	4	85-0078	28th BW, *Heavy Metal*, crashed near Alzada, Montana, 19 September 1997
66	5	86-0106	96th BW, *Lone Wolf*, crashed near Van Horn, Texas, 30 November 1992
74	5	86-0114	28th BW, *Live Free or Die*, crashed in Indian Ocean, 12 December 2001

MUSEUM AND GATE GUARD AIRCRAFT

Aircraft production number	Lot	Serial number	Name and location
2	2	83-0065	*Star of Abilene* – Dyess AFB
3	2	83-0066	*Ole' Puss* – Mountain Home AFB
7	2	83-0070	*7Wishes* – Hill AFB
8	2	83-0071	*Spit Fire* – Tinker AFB
11	3	84-0051	*Boss Hawg* – Wright Patterson AFB

APPENDIX B

B-1B COMBAT PARTICIPATION

OPERATION *DESERT FOX*

17-20 December 1998 – 4404th Wing (Provisional) – elements of the 37th and 9th BSs

OPERATION *NOBLE ANVIL*

24 March to 20 June 1999 – 16th AEW – elements of the 77th and 37th BSs

OPERATION *NORTHERN WATCH*

1 December 2000 to 28 February 2001 – 1st AEW – 34th BS as an on-call element

1 March to 30 May 2001 – 3rd AEF – 34th BS as an on-call element

1 June to 31 August 2001 – 5th AEF – 34th BS as an on-call element from 1 August

1 September to 30 November 2001 – 7th AEF – 34th BS as an on-call element

OPERATION *SOUTHERN WATCH*

1 December 2000 to 28 February 2001 – 2nd AEF – 9th BS as an assigned part of the Combat Air Force (CAF) and the 34th BS as an on-call element

1 March to 30 May 2001 – 4th AEF – 9th BS as an assigned part of the CAF and 34th BS as an on-call element

1 June to 31 August 2001 – 6th AEF – 128th ANG BS and 127th ANG BS as an assigned part of the CAF

1 September to 30 November 2001 – 8th AEF – 37th BS as an assigned part of the CAF and 34th BS as an on-call element

1 December 2001 to 28 February 2002 – 10th AEF – 77th BS as an assigned part of the CAF

OPERATIONS *ENDURING FREEDOM* AND *IRAQI FREEDOM*

Circa September 2001 to November 2005 – 405th AEW – the USAF is highly reticent to discuss the precise movements of B-1B units through Diego Garcia, Thumrait and Guam, the bases from which the bombers have been operating during these campaigns. However, throughout the past four years the 405th AEW has included elements from the 9th, 13th, 28th, 34th and 37th BSs, along with the now-re-rolled 128th ANG BS

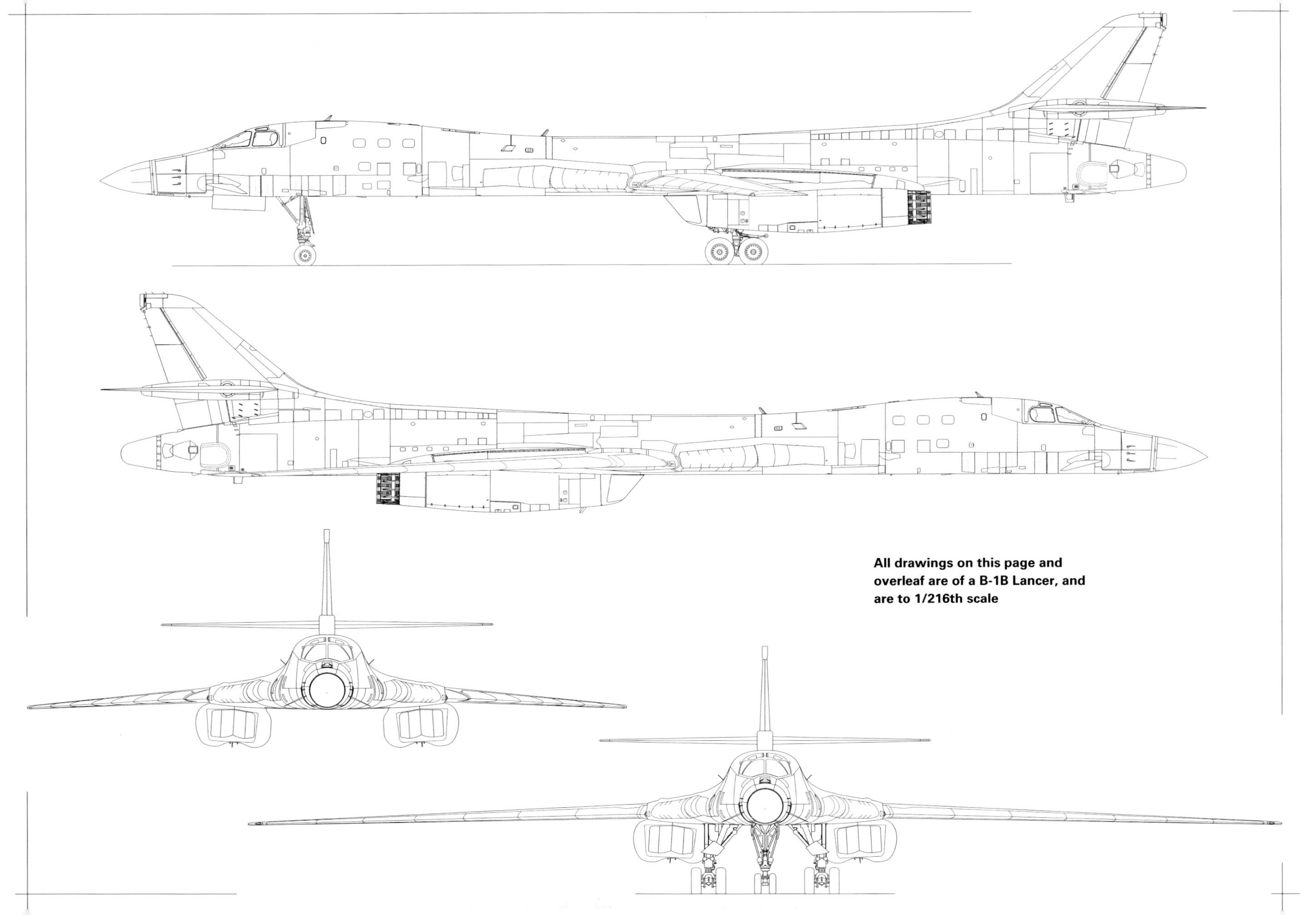

All drawings on this page and overleaf are of a B-1B Lancer, and are to 1/216th scale

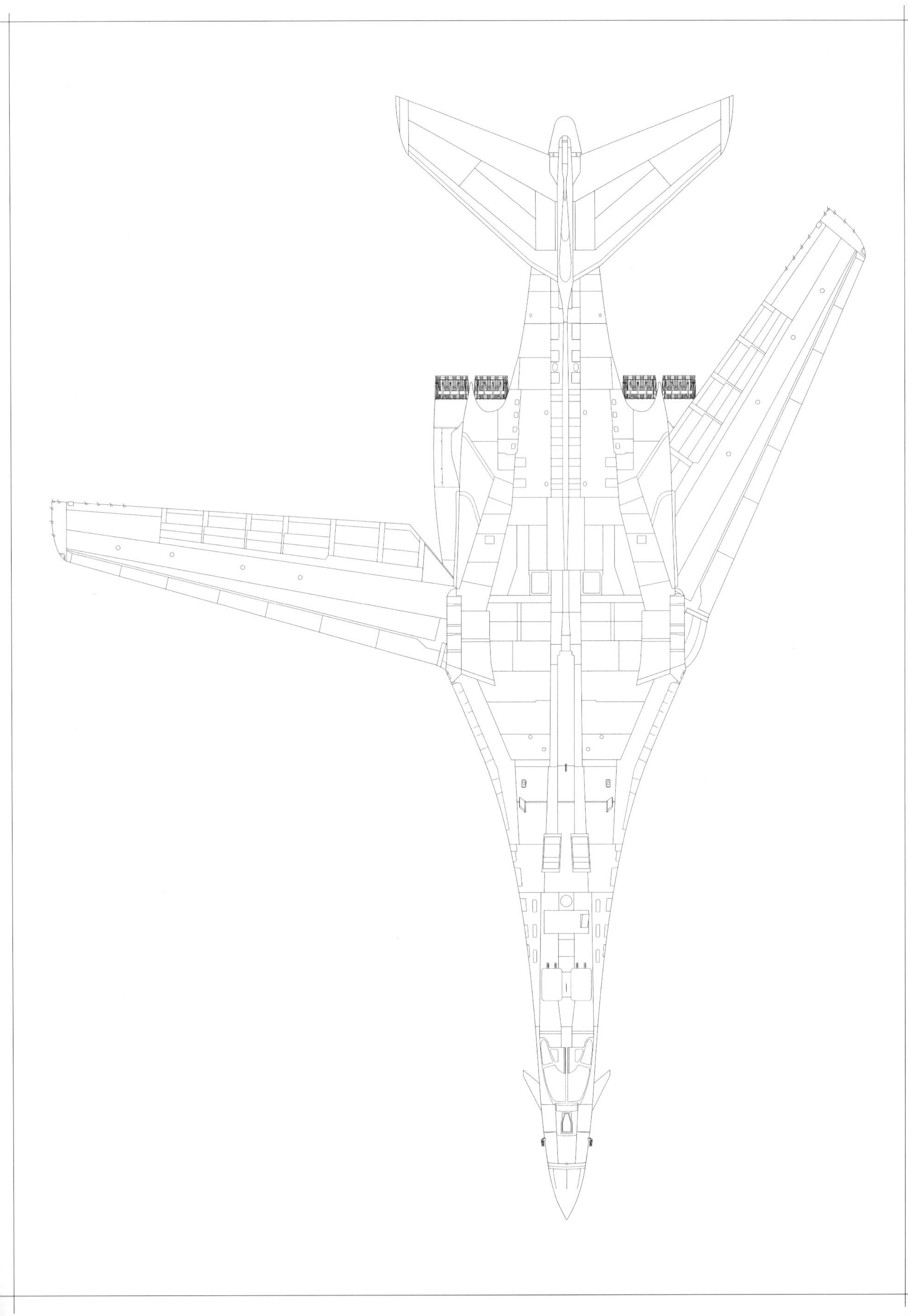

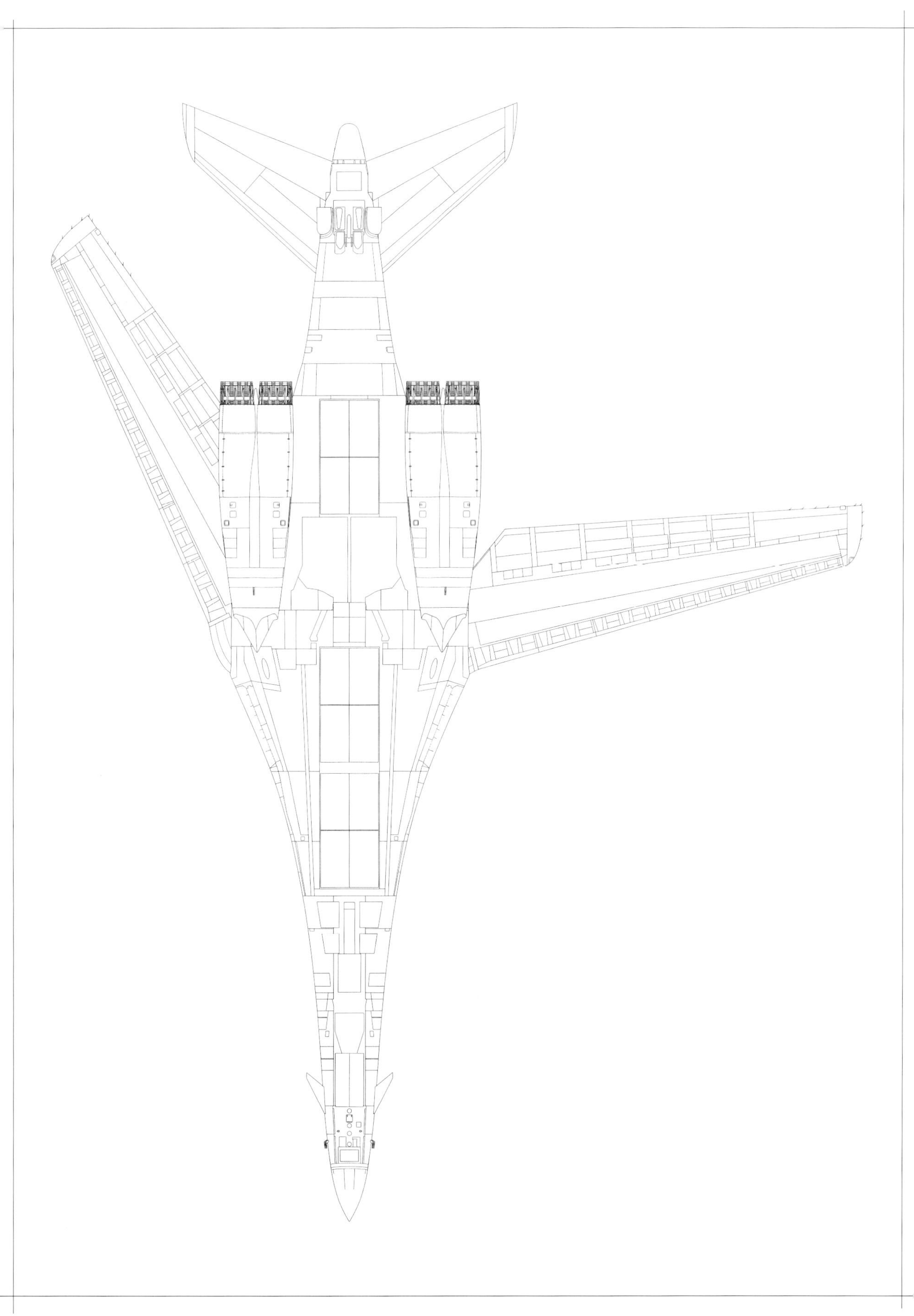

COLOUR PLATES

1

B-1B 85-0060 *DAKOTA POSSE* of the 34th BS/ 28th BW, Ellsworth AFB, 2005

85-0060 has changed identity on three occasions, having previously been called *Night Hawk*, *Rolling Thunder* and *Reach out and Touch Someone* during its service with the 127th BS at McConnell AFB, Kansas, prior to the unit switching to the air refuelling mission with the arrival of KC-135Rs. It is common knowledge that the Lancer was built to attack the former Soviet Union during the last years of the Cold War, but on 19 August 2005 this aircraft flew to the MAKS airshow at Zhukovsky, just outside Moscow. It became the first 'Bone' to participate in the event in the process, and to visit the home of its former adversary. The aircraft was commanded by Capt Steve Jones, who was quoted at the time as saying 'it's an honour to fly the first B-1B into Russia. We're all humbled that the Russians invited us to the airshow and are allowing us to participate'. This aircraft was the 20th B-1B delivered to the USAF.

2

B-1B 85-0062 *UNCAGED* of the 9th BS/7th BW, Dyess AFB, 2002

On 20 August 2002 this aircraft became the second B-1B Lancer to be retired to the AMARC at Davis-Monthan AFB, Arizona. The bomber was preceded by fellow Dyess Lancer 84-0065, which had arrived at the facility 24 hours earlier. The delivery of the aircraft to the AMARC was the first step in the consolidation of the Lancer fleet which will eventually see a total of 24 aircraft withdrawn from service and sent to the facility. Ten of the aircraft are to be held in storage, while the remaining fourteen will be cannibalised for spare parts. Previously called *Sky Dancer*, this aircraft was the 22nd Lancer delivered to the USAF.

3

B-1B 85-0066 *No Antidote II* of the 37th BS/ 28th BW, Ellsworth AFB, 2004

Previously known as *Special Delivery*, *Mis[sic] Behavin*, *Deadwood Express*, *Missouri Miss*, *Badlands Bomber*, *On Defense* and *Prowler*, this aircraft has always been assigned to the 28th BW. Like its *DAKOTA POSSE* sibling, *No Antidote II* has worn plenty of different names and nose-art during its two decades of service. This aircraft was the 26th Lancer to be delivered to the USAF.

4

B-1B 85-0072 *Polarized* of the 9th BS/7th BW, Dyess AFB, 2005

If ever there was an ironic name for a Lancer, then this was it. Its chilly monicker came from its participation in the '70 Degrees North' training mission, which it performed on 14 April 1987. The aircraft flew a test sortie to the Arctic with the aim of validating the aircraft's mission systems in northern areas. A year later, the aircraft flew south for Exercise *Distant Mariner 88*, which was held between 10-22 May 1988. This event tested the jet's navigation system as it crossed the International Dateline and the considerably warmer equator.

5

B-1B 85-0073 *DARK KNIGHT* of the 13th BS/ 7th BW, Dyess AFB, 1999

Arriving at the 7th BW on 21 January 1987, this aircraft was the 33rd B-1B to be delivered to the USAF, but only the second Lancer to equip the wing. The jet was also the fourth bomber to obtain the Block D upgrade, and was known as one of the 'Fast 7' aircraft (after the first seven Lancers to be designated as Block D airframes). It participated in ONA, but returned to the CONUS on 26 April, just under a month after it had arrived at Fairford. The bomber had previously carried the names *Wings of Freedom* and *Cerberus*.

6

B-1B 85-0077 *SCREAMIN EAGLE* of the 77th BS/ 28th BW, Ellsworth AFB, 2005

Although now named after the legendary Harley Davidson motorcycle, like most Lancers, this aircraft has changed its identity on numerous occasions. It was previously known as *Bones*, *Jap Happy*, *Hamton* and *Pride of South Dakota*. Presently the command jet of the 77th BS, it was the 37th Lancer to be delivered to the USAF.

7

B-1B 85-0079 *MASTER OF DISASTER* of the 77th BS/28th BW, Ellsworth AFB, 2005

The Lancer is no stranger to training initiatives, and in September 2002 this aircraft took part in the world-famous, annual, *Red Flag* exercises at Nellis AFB, Nevada. The exercise trains pilots from NATO and allied countries for real combat scenarios. The 39th 'Bone' delivered to the USAF, and a veteran of OEF, *MASTER OF DISASTER* has previously worn the names *Warrior's Dream*, *Classy Lady* and *Deadwood Dealer*.

8

B-1B 85-0083 *Overnight Delivery* of the 34th BS/ 28th BW, Ellsworth AFB, 1999

The third aircraft to obtain the Block D upgrade, and a veteran of ONA, this highly reliable 'Bone' distinguished itself by spending almost two months at the RAF's Gloucestershire base during the Balkans campaign, before finally returning to Ellsworth for maintenance. Previously known as *Dark Star*, 85-0083 was the 43rd Lancer to be delivered to the USAF.

9

B-1B 85-0085 *INTIMIDATOR* of the 37th BS/ 28th BW, Ellsworth AFB, 2005

The 45th B-1B delivered to the USAF, this bomber has had a rather chequered service career to date. In 1996 it suffered intermittent electrical power failures during an Operational Flight Check. A diagnosis of the aircraft at the Oklahoma City Air Logistics Center (OCALC) at Tinker AFB, Oklahoma, revealed that it was suffering the repeated failure of several electrical components which were eventually stripped out and replaced. The bomber remained out-of-service until January 1997. It was previously named *America's No 1* and *Brute Force*.

10

B-1B 85-0087 *SCREAMIN for VENGEANCE* of the 77th BS/28th BW, Ellsworth AFB, 2003

The 47th 'Bone' delivered to the USAF, this aircraft is also a *Red Flag* veteran, having participated in the exercise during August 2003. The jet joined three of its siblings for the manoeuvres, and they all operated from Nellis AFB, rather than from their Ellsworth home. All aircraft arrived for Period Two of the exercise from 16 to 29 August. Bearing *Judas Priest*-inspired nose art, this aircraft was previously called *Gremlin* and *Stars and Stripes*.

11

B-1B 85-0091 *FREEDOM'S VENGEANCE* of the 77th BS/28th BW, Ellsworth AFB, 1999

An historic B-1B in that it was the first of the 'Fast 7' aircraft to arrive at Ellsworth AFB after it had undergone its modifications on 29 October 1998, this jet was despatched to RAF Fairford in the spring of 1999 for operations in the Balkans. The 51st Lancer delivered to the USAF, 85-0091, like many of its contemporaries, has worn other names. It was originally called *Thor* and then *Hellcat*.

12

B-1B 86-0094 *Night Hawk* of the 37th BS/7th BW, Ellsworth AFB, 2000

Demonstrating how necessary the fuel management system is onboard the B-1B, *Night Hawk* suffered a mishap on 22 October 2000 while on the ramp at Ellsworth. A defective fuel pump allowed fuel to migrate from the forward fuel tank to the aft section of the aircraft, which in turn altered the centre-of-gravity parameters and caused the 'Bone' to come to rest on its tail. The 54th Lancer received by the USAF, it has only ever carried the name *Night Hawk*.

13

B-1B 86-0095 *DAKOTA DEMOLITION* of the 77th BS/28th BW Ellsworth AFB, 2003

Along with its sister aircraft *Ace in the hole*, *DAKOTA DEMOLITION* flew all the way from Ellsworth AFB to Waterkloof AFB for the South African International Air Show on 8-9 September 2000. A veteran of 11 missions in OIF, the bomber had also seen action in OEF. Previously named *Mistique* and *Undecided*, 86-0095 was the 55th B-1B delivered to the USAF.

14

B-1B 86-0099 *HAULIN' ASS* of the 37th BS/ 28th BW, Ellsworth AFB, 2004

The 59th B-1B delivered to the USAF, this aircraft was formerly known as *Ghost Rider* before its name was changed to *HAULIN' ASS*. Involved in live Mk 82 bomb trials in the mid 1990s, this jet subsequently dropped ordnance for real on targets in both Afghanistan and Iraq during the Global War On Terror.

15

B-1B 86-0103 *The Reluctant DRAGON* of the 9th BS/7th BW, Dyess AFB, 2004

Named after the hero of Kenneth Grahame's 1898 children's book in which a boy tries to persuade a shy, poetry-writing Dragon to become scary, this aircraft was the 63rd 'Bone' to be delivered to the USAF. On 6 June 1994 it took part in a 50-aircraft flypast of Omaha beach in Normandy to commemorate the 50th Anniversary of Operation *Overlord*. It was to be joined by its sibling 84-0057 *Hellion*, although this was prevented by bad weather. 86-0103 has previously borne the names *Huntress* and *Lovely Lady*.

16

B-1B 86-0108 *ALIEN WITH AN ATTITUDE* of the 28th BS/7th BW, Dyess AFB, 2005

On 19 June 1998, 86-0108 was part of a team of six Lancers that participated in NATO Exercise *Central Enterprise*. Deployed to RAF Fairford, this live-fire event was designed to test the integrated air defence systems of Western Europe. B-1Bs would fly in a strike package, escorted by F-16s and Tornados, while being marshalled by E-3 AWACS aircraft. They would then be 'attacked' by aggressor units of F-16s, F-4s, Tornados and MiG-29s. Previously christened *Hawk*, this aircraft was the 68th 'Bone' delivered to the USAF.

17

B-1B 86-0109 *SPECTRE* of the 28th BS/7th BW, Dyess AFB, 1998

Taking the war to the enemy, *SPECTRE* was one of four aircraft despatched to Oman to perform missions during ODF in 1998. The jet did not arrive in-theatre until 20 December, however, which meant that it was too late to participate in any of the strikes on Iraqi targets. Despite failing to drop any bombs, the B-1B's movement to southwest Asia undoubtedly sent a message to the Iraqi dictator that the United States was prepared to use 'heavy metal' to finish the job. Known only as *SPECTRE* during almost two decades of service with the USAF, this aircraft was the 69th Lancer delivered.

18

B-1B 86-0111 *Ace in the hole* of the 37th BS/ 28th BW, Ellsworth AFB, 2005

Formerly *Dakota Lightning*, this aircraft set a series

of time-to-height records shortly after becoming the 71st Lancer to be delivered to the USAF. While it did not participate in either ODF or ONA, it has since seen plenty of action over Afghanistan and Iraq.

19

B-1B 86-0113 *JAGGED EDGE* of the 37th BS/ 28th BW, Ellsworth AFB, 2003

Along with 86-0096, *JAGGED EDGE* participated in NATO's Exercise *Clean Hunter* in the summer of 2001. This initiative was designed to improve coordination in live air operations. Since then, the bomber has been an active participant in OIF in 2003. The 73rd Lancer delivered to the USAF, it was previously known as *Charon, Viper* and *Dakota Reveille*.

20

B-1B 86-0114 *LIVE FREE OR DIE* of the 37th BS/ 28th BW, Ellsworth AFB, 2001

Outbound from Diego Garcia on the night of 12 December 2001, heading for Afghanistan, this aircraft suffered a serious systems failure just 100 miles north of its base and subsequently crashed. The official report into the accident concluded that the aircraft's onboard electrical generator may have played a part in its demise. An 'oil hot' warning was displayed on the cockpit avionics panel, causing the crew to shut down an engine to bring the oil temperature back to a safe level. The crew also shut off the electrical generator and decided to return to Diego Garcia. It was whilst heading home that a second generator failed, cutting the power to the aircraft's navigation instruments. Despite switching on emergency power generators, the jet's navigation instruments were displaying insufficient information about the aircraft's altitude and position for the crew to keep the B-1B in level flight. Indeed, during the last minute of the mission the bomber lost 20,000 ft. After 15 minutes of wrestling with the aircraft's controls, the crew decided to eject at an altitude of 15,000 ft over the Indian Ocean. They escaped serious injury and were rescued by the US Navy destroyer USS *Russell* (DDG-59). The remains of the aircraft rest at the bottom of the Indian Ocean. This particular B-1B (along with 86-0119) had the distinction of making the first ever appearance of a Lancer at the RAF Mildenhall airshow in May 1989. Both aircraft were assigned to the 46th BS/319th BW at Grand Forks AFB, North Dakota, at the time – the 319th swapped its B-1Bs for KC-135Rs in the Autumn of 1993, becoming the 319th Air Refueling Wing in the process. 86-0114 had previously worn the names *Wolfhound* and *Dakota Drifter*.

21

B-1B 86-0120 *IRON HORSE* of the 9th BS/7th BW, Dyess AFB, 2005

The 80th B-1B to be delivered to the USAF, this aircraft, like many of its brethren, sat out operations in the Balkans and Iraq during 1998-99. The bomber was in the forefront of the action in Afghanistan and Iraq, however. 86-0120 was previously called *Mad Dawg*.

22

B-1B 86-0121 *Symphony of DESTRUCTION* of the 37th BS/28th BW, Ellsworth AFB, 2003

The 81st B-1B delivered to the USAF, this aircraft participated in aircrew bottom-bailout tests soon after its delivery. Some 15 years later, 86-0121 became the very first aircraft to go 'downtown' over Baghdad during OIF. It became the record-holder for the longest OIF combat sortie undertaken by a B-1B in the process, the jet having taken off from Guam to perform its 21.7-hour marathon mission. During the course of the mission, the crew performed a total of six aerial refuellings. This aircraft has carried the names *Exterminator, Terminator, Zeppelin* and *Maiden America* at various stages in its service career.

23

B-1B 86-0123 *"LET'S ROLL"* of the 77th BS/ 28th BW, Ellsworth AFB, 2002

The B-1B is a rare visitor to the UK except during airshows in the summer months. However, in May 2001 four aircraft were stationed at RAF Mildenhall en route to an exercise in Oman. At the time, this aircraft was named *High Noon*, although it would later be christened *"LET'S ROLL"* after the final words uttered by Todd Beamer before he and other passengers rushed the terrorists on one of the hijacked aircraft during the 11 September 2001 attacks. This was the 83rd Lancer to be delivered to the USAF, and it has also worn the names *Molester* and *Lester*.

24

B-1B 86-0124 *GEORGIA GUARDIAN* of the 34th BS/28th BW, Ellsworth, 2005

The 84th B-1B to be delivered to the USAF, *GEORGIA GUARDIAN* had the distinction of performing the very last flight made by an ANG-manned Lancer on 22 June 2002. Prior to that, the aircraft had been a frequent transatlantic flyer, first visiting the UK on 25 August 1988 when it made its debut public appearance in the static park during the RAF Lakenheath airshow. 86-0124 has previously carried the names *Penetrator* and *Winged Thunder*.

25

B-1B 86-0125 *Swift JUSTICE* of the 77th BS/ 28th BW, Ellsworth AFB, 2005

Another veteran of OIF, this aircraft completed eight missions during the conflict. Previously known as *Shack Attack*, and having served for several years with the ANG prior to joining the 28th BW, it also saw combat over Afghanistan. 86-0125 was the 85th Lancer to be delivered to the USAF.

26

B-1B 86-0128 *Fury 1* of the 37th BS/28th BW, Ellsworth AFB, 2002

Now a resident of the AMARC, this aircraft initially conducted climatic tests upon its delivery to the USAF in 1987. The bomber was badly damaged on

14 October 1990 when it suffered an uncontained blade failure in its number one engine during a training sortie, forcing the crew to make an emergency night landing at Pueblo, California. Dramatically, the accident caused the engine to completely break away from the aircraft and crash to the ground, fortunately without causing any damage. The bomber was later ferried with three engines to the OCALC for repairs. As its brethren were preparing for their attacks on targets in Iraq, this aircraft was being delivered to AMARC – it arrived on 31 March 2003, and now carries the number AABT0015. The jet also carried the names *The Hawk*, *Miss Behavin*, *Boss* and *Pony Soldier* at various stages during its 16-year career.

27

B-1B 86-0129 *Black Widow* of the 34th BS/ 28th BW, Ellsworth AFB, 1999

This aircraft is a veteran of service with the 127th ANG BS prior to its arrival at Ellsworth after the reconsolidation of B-1B Lancer basing. Formerly known as *Pegasus*, it spent just under six weeks at RAF Fairford during ONA, before returning home. 86-0129 was the 89th Lancer delivered to the USAF.

28

B-1B 86-0130 *BAD COMPANY* of the 28th BS/ 7th BW, Dyess AFB, 2005

One of the last Lancers to be delivered to the USAF, *BAD COMPANY* was the 90th 'Bone' to be produced by Rockwell International. Although failing to participate in either ODF or ONA, the aircraft (which was previously know as *The Rose*) has since been involved in operations over southwest Asia as part of the Global War on Terror.

29

B-1B 86-0133 *Old Crow Express III/Memphis Belle* of the 28th BS/7th BW, Dyess AFB, 2001

Formerly an aircraft of the Georgia ANG's 116th BW, this B-1B carries two names. Along with its *Old Crow Express III* monicker, it was also christened *Memphis Belle* at a ceremony held at Robins AFB, Georgia, on 28 July 2000. The latter name was originally applied to the first B-17 Flying Fortress to complete 25 missions with the Eighth Air Force in World War 2. Previously called *Big Bird*, *The Outlaw* and *Black Hills Bandit*, *Old Crow Express III* was the 93rd Lancer to be delivered to the USAF.

30

B-1B 86-0138 *SEEK AND DESTROY* of the 37th BS/28th BW, Dyess AFB, 2003

One of the most historic of all B-1B Lancers, this bomber was sent to execute the famous OIF 'head shot' against Saddam Hussein and his two sons, who were reportedly dining at a restaurant in the suburbs of Baghdad on 7 April 2003. The weapons mix used by the aircraft, consisting of 2000-lb GBU-31(V)1/(V)2 JDAM, was specifically chosen to minimise collateral damage on the ground, given that the target was located in a residential area. After being tasked, the crew located the target, planned an escape route from the attack, surveyed nearby enemy air defences and maintained contact with airborne and ground controllers. They also selected the weapons which would be used in the strike, and 'dialled in' the Global Positioning System coordinates – all in under ten minutes. This aircraft was the 98th Lancer to be delivered to the USAF, and had previously been called *Easyrider Too* and *Grand Illusion II*.

INDEX

References to illustrations are shown in **bold**. Plates are shown with page and caption locators in brackets.